sci Fair

j

Health Science Projects About
Heredity

Titles in the **Science Projects** *series*

Health Science Projects About Anatomy and Physiology
0-7660-1440-1

Science Projects About Light
0-89490-529-5

Health Science Projects About Nutrition
0-7660-1442-8

Science Projects About Math
0-89490-950-9

Health Science Projects About Psychology
0-7660-1439-8

Science Projects About Methods of Measuring
0-7660-1169-0

Health Science Projects About Your Senses
0-7660-1437-1

Science Projects About Physics in the Home
0-89490-948-7

Health Science Projects About Sports Performance
0-7660-1441-X

Science Projects About the Physics of Sports
0-7660-1167-4

Science Fair Projects—Planning, Presenting, Succeeding
0-89490-949-5

Science Projects About the Physics of Toys and Game
0-7660-1165-8

Science Projects About Chemistry
0-89490-531-7

Science Projects About Plants
0-89490-952-5

Science Projects About Electricity and Magnets
0-89490-530-9

Science Projects About the Science Behind Magic
0-7660-1164-X

Science Projects About the Environment and Ecology
0-89490-951-7

Science Projects About Solids Liquids, and Gases
0-7660-1168-2

Science Projects About the Human Body
0-89490-443-4

Science Projects About Sound
0-7660-1166-6

Science Projects About Kitchen Chemistry
0-89490-953-3

Science Projects About Temperature and Heat
0-89490-534-1

Science Projects About Weather
0-89490-533-3

Health Science Projects About Heredity

Robert Gardner

Science Projects

Enslow Publishers, Inc.

40 Industrial Road	PO Box 38
Box 398	Aldershot
Berkeley Heights, NJ 07922	Hants GU12 6BP
USA	UK

http://www.enslow.com

Library of Congress Cataloging-in-Publication Data

Gardner, Robert, 1929–
    Health science projects about heredity / Robert Gardner.
        p. cm. — (Science projects)
    Includes bibliographical references and index.
    ISBN 0-7660-1438-X (alk. paper)
    1. Heredity—Juvenile literature. 2. Biology projects—Juvenile literature. [1.
Heredity—Experiments. 2. Genetics—Experiments. 3. Experiments. 4. Science projects.]
I. Title.
QH437.5 .G37 2001
576.5'078—dc21
                                                        00-010759

Printed in the United States of America

10 9 8 7 6 5 4 3 2

To Our Readers: We have done our best to make sure all Internet addresses in this book
were active and appropriate when we went to press. However, the author and the publisher
have no control over and assume no liability for the material available on those Internet sites
or on other Web sites they may link to. Any comments or suggestions can be sent by e-mail
to comments@enslow.com or to the address on the back cover.

Illustration credits: Stephen F. Delisle, pp. 16, 24, 35, 36, 40, 43, 63, 79, 86, 95,
96, 99, 101; Enslow Publishers, Inc., pp. 20, 26, 29, 31, 39, 48, 51, 52, 53, 55, 58,
69, 72, 75, 76, 81; Gary Koellhoffer, Crooked Grin Design, pp. 82, 88.

Cover illustration: Jerry McCrea (foreground); © Corel Corporation
(background).

Contents

Introduction 7

1. The Emergence of Genetics,
the Science of Heredity 11
    1-1* A Model to Explain Mendel's Initial Experiments . . 19
    1-2* The Role of Probability in Heredity 23
    1-3* Modeling the Inheritance of
           Two Independent Traits 28

2. Mendel, Genes, Chromosomes,
and Models 33
    2-1* A Look at Chromosomes 38
    2-2* A Model of Mitosis 39
    2-3* A Model of Meiosis 42
    2-4* Experimenting with *Drosophila melanogaster* 47

3. Heredity and Family 50
    3-1 Tracing an Inherited Trait 55
    3-2* Making Your Own Family Tree 56
    3-3 Tracing Eye Color in Your Family 57
    3-4 Taste, PTC, and Genetics 58
    3-5 Taste, Thiourea, and Genetics 60
    3-6 Taste, Sodium Benzoate, and Genetics 61
    3-7 The Inheritance of Other Human Traits 62
    3-8 Eye Color and Genes 64
    3-9 The Inheritance of Hair Color 65
    3-10*Inheritance of Human Blood Types 68

4. Genes That Are Linked 71
    4-1 A Model for Linked Genes 74
    4-2 A Model of Sex Determination 78

*appropriate ideas for science fair project

4-3* A Sex-Linked Trait in Humans 84

4-4   The Inheritance of the Length of Index Fingers . . . 86

4-5* Gender and Probability 87

5. The Chemistry of Genes **92**

5-1   A Three-Dimensional Model of DNA 101

5-2* Gene Coding and a Mutation 102

5-3* A Model to Show How DNA Controls
      the Making of Proteins 104

**6. Nature vs. Nurture, Cloning,
and Genetic Engineering** **106**

6-1   Seeds and the Effects of Nurture on Nature 108

6-2* Cloning, Food, and Humans 113

Glossary **116**

List of Suppliers **121**

Further Reading **123**

Internet Addresses **125**

Index **126**

*appropriate ideas for science fair project

Introduction

The science projects and experiments in this book involve heredity, genetics, and family. Heredity is the transmission of characteristic traits, such as eye, hair, and skin color, from generation to generation. Genetics is the science that explores how those traits are passed from parents to offspring. As you will find, genes make up the chromosomes found in the nuclei of egg and sperm cells. They are the mechanisms for transmitting the information needed for new offspring to develop their characteristic traits. They also provide the codes that direct the many chemical and physical changes needed to maintain life. Chemically, genes are made of DNA (deoxyribonucleic acid), the blueprint from which organisms are made and that regulates all life processes.

To obtain data for some of the projects in this book, you will have to observe and talk to members of your family and the families of your friends. In some projects you may need people to help you with experiments because more than one pair of hands may be required. Since some of the experiments will take a significant amount of time, try to choose friends who are patient. It might be best if you work with people who enjoy experimenting as much as you do.

As you do these projects, you will find it useful to record your ideas, procedures, data, and anything you can conclude from your experiments in a notebook. In that way, you can keep track of the information you gather and the conclusions you reach. This will make it easy to refer to completed experiments as you do later projects.

Science Fairs

Some of the projects in this book might be appropriate for a science fair. Those projects are indicated with an asterisk (*). However, judges at science fairs do not reward projects or experiments that are simply copied from a book. For example, a model of a cell would probably not impress judges unless it was done in a novel or creative way. A model of a cell that would undergo cell division while judges watched would receive more consideration than a rigid papier-mâché model.

Science fair judges tend to reward creative thought and imagination. However, it is difficult to be creative or imaginative unless you are really interested in your project, so choose something that appeals to you. Consider, too, your own ability and the cost of materials needed for the project.

If you decide to use a project found in this book for a science fair, you will need to find ways to modify or extend it. This should not be difficult, because as you do these projects new ideas for experiments will come to mind. These new experiments are what will make excellent science fair projects because they spring from your own mind and are interesting to you.

If you decide to enter a science fair and have never done so before, you should read some of the books listed in the further reading section. The references that deal specifically with science fairs will provide plenty of helpful hints and lots of useful information that will enable you to avoid the pitfalls that sometimes plague first-time entrants. You will learn how to prepare appealing reports that include charts and graphs, how to set up and display your work, how to present your project, and how to relate to judges and visitors.

Safety First

Most of the projects included in this book are perfectly safe. However, the following safety rules are well worth reading before you start any project.

1. Do any experiments or projects, whether from this book or of your own design, under the supervision of a science teacher or other knowledgeable adult.

2. Read all instructions carefully before proceeding with a project. If you have questions, check with your supervisor before going any further.

3. Maintain a serious attitude while conducting experiments. Fooling around can be dangerous to you and to others.

4. Wear approved safety goggles when you are doing anything that might cause injury to your eyes.

5. Do not eat or drink while experimenting.

6. Have a first-aid kit nearby while you are experimenting.

7. Do not put your fingers or any object in electrical outlets.

8. Never experiment with household electricity except under the supervision of a knowledgeable adult.

9. Never touch a lit high-wattage bulb. Lightbulbs produce light but they also produce heat.

10. Many substances are poisonous. Do not taste them unless instructed to do so.

1

The Emergence of Genetics, the Science of Heredity

All humans belong to the same species: *Homo sapiens*. As *Homo sapiens*, we share many features. We have all the characteristics of mammals and of primates. Like all primates, our teeth are adapted to a general diet, and our eyes are at the front of our heads so that each eye has the same view from a slightly different angle. This eye placement gives us a three-dimensional view of the world and therefore good depth perception. The upper sides of our fingers and toes are covered by flat nails rather than claws. Our fingers and toes are flexible and capable of a wide range of movement.

We also differ from other primates in some ways. Our big toes are not opposable (they cannot touch the other toes) and are not splayed (turned out) as they are in most primates. But our thumbs are almost as long as our other digits (fingers). This allows us to grip and manipulate tools with great precision. We walk on two feet, not four. Finally, our brains are three times as large as those of chimpanzees—our closest primate relatives. Our big brains enable us to make extensive use of language, the basis for human culture.

Humans are unique in many ways. We make large-scale use of tools, we can control fire, we share food, we find or build protective shelters, and we transmit more than genes to our offspring. Because of our extensive use of language, we transmit beliefs and ideas from generation to generation. All these factors are parts of the main human advantage over other species, which is culture and the social structure that accompanies it. But culture seems to be the result of two things: a highly developed language and a large brain. It is doubtful that we ever had one without the other. Associated with culture, and perhaps also with language, brain size, and the capacity to convey ideas with symbols, is art. In fact, art, in the form of the drawings and paintings found in ancient cave dwellings, may have been our first attempt to convey ideas by the use of symbols.

The physical traits that characterize humans must be inherited because we find them persisting through many generations. But language, art, tools, the shelters we build, and the way we organize families and behave toward one another are not inherited. They differ from culture to culture. For example, many Native American tribes were nomadic. They followed their food sources and built shelters that could be moved easily from place to place. The Europeans who came to America were predominantly farmers. They built permanent shelters and raised crops, cattle, pigs, and sheep near their shelters on land they claimed to own. The Native Americans had no concept of owning land. It was not part of their culture.

Since the dawn of agriculture some 10,000 years ago, some human cultures have tried to improve the heredity of the domestic plants and animals they use for food. They did this by selecting the best organisms for breeding. Knowing that offspring resemble their parents, they selected for mating the goats that produced the most milk, the cattle that provided the most meat or milk, and the corn that produced the largest ears. Over centuries, their selective breeding led to plants and animals that were more productive. In some cases, however, particularly when the animals they bred were closely related, the results were unsatisfactory: the offspring were born dead or sickly. It took nearly 10 millennia for people to understand why selective breeding worked in some cases and not in others.

Early Theories of Heredity

More than 2,500 years ago, Pythagoras, an early Greek philosopher also known for his work in mathematics, had a theory about the transmission of characteristics. He argued that the hereditary traits of all animals, including humans, are carried in the male's semen. According to Pythagoras, semen, once inside the female's uterus, developed into a baby during gestation (the length of a pregnancy).

Two centuries later, Aristotle, another Greek philosopher, reasoned that because children resemble their mothers as well as their fathers, both males and females must contribute hereditary factors. He believed that both sexes produce semen, which is derived from their blood. According to Aristotle, male and female semen unite in the uterus to form an embryo that grows into a baby during gestation.

Later, people believed that each body organ provided semen with "vapors" that contained the hereditary factors for that body part. However, in the seventeenth century, Antoni van Leeuwenhoek (1632–1723), while looking at semen through his simple microscope, saw sperm cells, or what he called animalcules. His discovery led people to believe that sperm transmit hereditary factors from father to offspring.

Others who examined sperm cells through microscopes claimed to see miniature humans—homunculi—curled up inside the sperm. This led to the belief that babies existed in a preformed state within sperm cells. In the warm and nourishing environment of the womb, these preformed embryos simply grew larger before being born.

At about the same time, others dissected animals and found swollen bodies on the ovaries of the females. These were correctly assumed to be eggs. This suggested that females transmit hereditary factors through their eggs, while males transmit theirs through sperm cells.

Pierre-Louis de Maupertuis (1698–1759) recognized that offspring often have physical characteristics that resemble those found in one or both parents. He proposed that tiny particles from all parts of the bodies of both parents are brought together at the time of conception. However, the factor for a particular feature from one parent, such as height or eye color, may dominate (hide) the corresponding factor from the other parent.

At about the time of the American revolution, a German biologist, Kaspar Friedrich Wolff (1733–1794), was studying chick embryos and other embryonic tissues under the microscope. He saw that no miniature versions of adult organs were present in an embryo. Over time, he observed that the unspecialized cells in an embryo change into muscle, nerve, blood, connective, and epithelial tissues. Wolff's work suggested that a sperm and an egg cell unite to form a single cell, a zygote (from the Greek word for yoked, or joined). The zygote then divides many times, forming a many-celled embryo. Eventually the cells become specialized, giving rise to tissues and organs that mature prior to birth.

Although Wolff's theory of embryonic development (epigenesis) was essentially correct, it was 1839 before it became widely accepted. By then, two German scientists, botanist Matthias Schleiden (1804–1881) and zoologist Theodor Schwann (1810–1882), had demonstrated that the cell is the fundamental unit of life in both plants and animals.

Exploring on Your Own

What is the famous mathematical theorem that bears Pythagoras' name?

How large is a human egg cell? How does the size of a human sperm cell compare with the size of a human egg?

Gregor Mendel, the Father of Genetics

By the middle of the nineteenth century, the idea that a sperm and egg cell combine to form a zygote that develops into a new organism during gestation had become widely accepted. However, the way hereditary traits are transmitted from one generation to the next remained a mystery.

Charles Darwin (1809–1882) wrote that evolution occurs because the great variety among members of a species makes some better suited for survival than others. However, he could not explain why organisms differ. Nor could he explain how traits are passed on from generation to generation.

It was Gregor Mendel (1822–1884), an Austrian monk, who first did experiments that led to the basic laws of genetics. Mendel, a botanist who was also trained in mathematics, began growing pea plants in the garden at his monastery in 1856. This was three years before Darwin published his book *The Origin of Species.*

Mendel's Initial Experiments

Mendel investigated, one at a time, seven traits he had observed in pea plants. These traits were height (tall or short), seed shape (round or wrinkled), color of the seed leaves or cotyledons (yellow or green), seed coats (clear or brown), pod shape (inflated or constricted), pod color (yellow or green), and position of pods on the stem (terminal or axial). Terminal pods form at the top of the stem, axial pods form along the sides of the stem. Figure 1 illustrates these traits.

Mendel began his experiments with true-breeding varieties— plants that had for many generations showed only one of the two forms for any of the seven traits he studied. He crossed (mated) true-breeding plants with plants of contrasting traits. These plants were known as the parent, or P_1, generation. To make these crosses, he

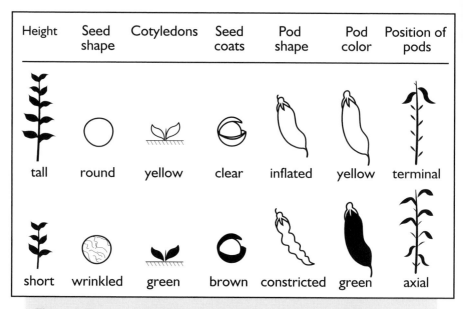

Height	Seed shape	Cotyledons	Seed coats	Pod shape	Pod color	Position of pods
tall	round	yellow	clear	inflated	yellow	terminal
short	wrinkled	green	brown	constricted	green	axial

Figure 1. The seven traits found in pea plants that were investigated by Gregor Mendel are illustrated in these drawings.

carefully removed the stamens from, say, the flowers of a tall plant and placed their pollen on the pistils of a short plant. He also removed the stamens from the flowers of short plants and placed their pollen grains on the pistils of tall plants. This prevented the plants from self-pollinating, which is normally the way pea plants reproduce. He would then cover the flowers to prevent any further pollination by wind or insects.

The seeds produced by the cross-pollinated flowers from the P_1 generation were planted and observed. The plants that grew from these seeds—known as the first filial, or F_1, generation—flowered and were allowed to self-pollinate. The seeds produced by the F_1 generation grew into the plants of the second filial, or F_2, generation.

Mendel's Results

When the P_1 generation was true-breeding tall plants crossed with true-breeding short plants, all the F_1 plants that grew from their seeds were tall. There were no short plants. However, the factor for shortness had not disappeared. When he allowed the F_1 plants to self-pollinate and produce the F_2 generation, the results were striking. Both tall and short plants grew from these seeds. The factor for shortness that had been hidden in the F_1 generation reappeared in one fourth of the F_2 plants. The other three fourths were tall, a ratio of 3:1.

When the plants of the F_2 generation reproduced by self-pollination, Mendel found that all the short plants were true-breeding: they produced only short offspring. Of the tall plants, one third were true-breeding; they produced only tall offspring. The other two thirds produced both tall and short plants in the same ratio (3:1) as their F_1 ancestors. Table 1 summarizes Mendel's results.

Mendel found similar results when he crossed plants for each of the other six contrasting traits he studied. His results for the F_1 and F_2 generations for each of the seven traits he studied are shown in Table 2. In all cases, the F_2 plants produced the same 3:1 pattern of offspring.

The results show that in the F_2 generation, one trait is three times as likely to appear as the other. The trait that appears three times as frequently is the same one that appears in all plants in the

Table 1. Mendel's results when he crossed true-breeding tall pea plants with true-breeding short pea plants (P_1 generation), and then allowed their offspring to self-pollinate.

Generation	Cross	Offspring from seeds
P_1	tall x short ⇒	F_1—all tall
F_1	tall x tall ⇒	F_2—3 tall:1 short
F_2	short x short ⇒	F_3—all short
	1/3 (tall x tall) ⇒	F_3—all tall
	2/3 (tall x tall) ⇒	F_3—3 tall:1 short

F_1 generation. Mendel referred to the trait that appeared three times more frequently in the F_2 generation as the dominant trait. A trait that disappeared in the F_1 generation, such as shortness, he called a recessive trait. When both traits were present in a seed, only the dominant one could be seen. It took precedence over the recessive trait. Thus, in pea plants, tallness is a dominant trait, while shortness is a recessive trait. From Table 2, can you identify the dominant and recessive trait in each of the other six characteristics Mendel investigated?

Table 2. Mendel's results for the F_1 and F_2 generations for each of seven traits inherited by pea plants. An X is used to indicate a cross (mating) between plants with contrasting traits, such as tallness and shortness).

P_1	F_1	F_2	Ratio
tall x short	all were tall	787 were round 277 were short	2.84:1
round x wrinkled seeds	all were round	5,474 were round 1,850 were wrinkled	2.96:1
yellow x green cotyledons	all were yellow	6,022 were yellow 2,001 were green	3.01:1
brown x clear seed coats	all were brown	705 were brown 224 were clear	3.15:1
inflated x constricted pods	all were inflated	882 were inflated 299 were constricted	2.95:1
green x yellow pods	all were green	428 were green 152 were yellow	2.82:1
axial x terminal pods	all were axial	651 were axial 207 were terminal	3.14:1

1-1*
A Model to Explain Mendel's Initial Experiments

Without reading any further, see if you can develop a model (theory) to explain the results of Mendel's experiments.

Now let's compare your model with Mendel's. The traits that Mendel studied are transmitted from one generation to the next. Consequently, he assumed that there are hereditary factors that are passed to the next generation through the plants' gametes (from the Greek *gamein*, "to marry"), which are the sperm cells in the pollen and the egg cells in the pistil.

Things you will need:

• 24 brown and 24 white bean seeds similar in size

• 2 paper cups

• notebook

• pen or pencil

You can represent the factor for tall pea plants with brown beans and the factor for short pea plants with white beans. Place two dozen brown beans in one paper cup. This cup represents the tall pea plant. Place an equal number of white beans in a second cup. This cup represents the short pea plant.

Since inheritable factors come from both parents, let's assume, as Mendel did, that in the P_1 generation the purebred tall plants have only the factor for tallness, represented by the brown beans. Purebred short plants have only the factor for shortness, represented by the white beans. Let's assume also, as Mendel did, that the F_1 generation receives only one factor for height from each parent (Figure 2).

In your physical model this can be done by taking one bean from each of the two cups and putting them together. Another way to do this is to make a Punnett square and let letters represent the inherited factors. Figure 2c shows how to make a Punnett square for the P_1 and the F_1 crosses where tallness is involved. The symbols representing the inherited factors for one parent are listed along one side of the square. The symbols representing the inherited factors

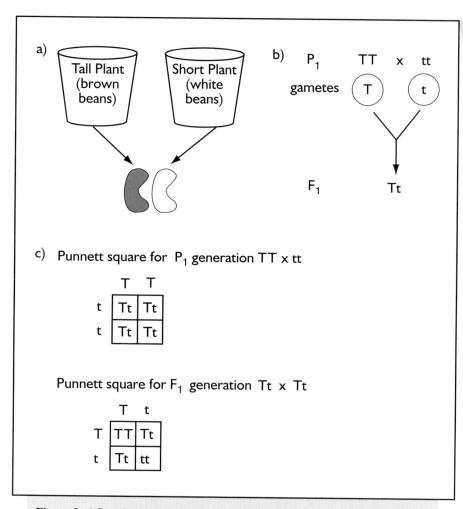

Figure 2. a) Pure breeding tall plants have only the factor for tallness. That factor is represented by brown beans. Pure breeding short plants have only the factor for shortness. That factor is represented by white beans. The F_1 generation receives one factor for height from each parent. Since the factor for tallness is a dominant factor, all the F_1 plants will be tall. b) The cross between tall and short plants can also be represented by symbols. Here, *T* represents the dominant factor for tallness, *t* represents the recessive factor for shortness. All gametes from the tall plant carry the factor *T*. All gametes from the short plant carry the factor *t*. The cells of the F_1 plants have both the *T* and the *t* factors. The plants are tall because tallness is a dominant factor. c) The diagrams show Punnett squares for the P_1 and F_1 generations. *T* is the factor for tall; *t* is the factor for short.

for the other parent are listed along the top. Each possible combination of inherited factors that can be found in the offspring are listed inside the square. For example, the first T on the top crossed with the first t on the side gives Tt in the top left box. By counting the number of times a combination appears in the squares, you can predict the likelihood of that trait appearing in the offspring.

As you can see from Figure 2a, Figure 2b, and the first Punnett square in Figure 2c, all the F_1 offspring will be tall. This is because the factor for tallness, represented by the brown bean or the capital letter T, is dominant over the factor for shortness, represented by the white bean or the small letter t. When the hereditary factors for both tall and short plants are present in a plant's cells, the plant will be tall.

What hereditary factors for height will be in the gametes produced by plants of the F_1 generation? What kind of offspring will be produced?

The second Punnett square shows that the inherited factors, T and t, can combine in three different ways: TT, Tt, and tt. Since T is dominant over t, 3 of every 4 F_1 offspring will be tall (TT, Tt, and Tt) and 1 will be short (tt).

To see if this works in a more concrete way, place one dozen each of dry brown beans and dry white beans in the same cup. Cover the cup with your hand and shake it to thoroughly mix the beans. Do the same with a second paper cup. Each cup contains the hereditary factors for height that can be in a gamete produced by an F_1 pea plant. Each cup represents a parent plant from the F_1 generation. Each bean represents a hereditary factor that can be found in a sperm or egg cell, the gametes.

Close your eyes and remove a bean (representing a factor for height) from one cup. This bean is the hereditary factor that will be in the sperm. Then repeat the procedure for the other cup. This is the hereditary factor that will be in the egg. The two beans together represent the hereditary factors that will be in the seed.

21

Record the result in your notebook. If you drew two brown beans, record it as TT, because the factors for height from both parents were for tallness. (The capital T shows that it is a dominant factor.) If you drew two white beans, record it as tt. (The small letter t shows that it is a recessive factor.) If you drew a brown bean and a white bean, record it as Tt. (This seed will produce a tall plant, but it also carries the factor for shortness.)

Return the beans to their respective cups and shake the cups again. Repeat the process of drawing one bean from each cup and recording the result 100 times. Be sure to return the beans to their respective cups and shake the cups after each drawing.

These paired factors illustrate the way factors would join to form 100 seeds of the next (F_2) generation. What would be the height of the plants produced by each of the seeds whose factors you recorded? How many will be tall? How many will be short? Based on your data, what percentage of the F_2 generation will be tall? What percentage will be short? Of those that are tall, what percentage will be true-breeding (two brown)? That is, what percentage will have only the hereditary factor for tallness? (Such plants are said to be *homozygous*—from the Greek words *homo*: "same," and *zygous*: "yoked"—because both factors are the same. Notice that all the short plants are homozygous.) What percentage will have a factor for both tall and short (Tt: one brown, one white)? (Such plants are said to be *heterozygous*—from the Greek word *hetero*: "different".)

How do the percentages of tall and short plants in the F_2 generation that you obtained in your experiment compare with Mendel's results (see Table 1)? Why might your ratios be different from his?

Exploring on Your Own

Is it reasonable to assume, as Mendel did, that only one member of each pair of hereditary factors gets into a gamete? If so, why is it reasonable? If not, why isn't it reasonable? Did Mendel's results confirm his assumption?

1-2*
The Role of Probability in Heredity

In the previous activity, you developed a model to explain the results of crossing a pure-breeding (homozygous—with the same inheritance factors) tall pea plant with a short plant. All members of the F_1 generation were tall. In the F_2 generation

Things you will need:

- 2 pennies, one bright and shiny and one tarnished and dull
- a friend
- pen or pencil
- notebook

you saw that we can expect three fourths of the plants to be tall (see Figure 2 and Table 2). However, we would expect only one third of those plants (one quarter of the total number of plants) to be homozygous for tallness. Two thirds of them (one half the total number of plants) can be expected to carry the recessive factor for shortness as well as the dominant factor for tallness. The probability of a (true-breeding [homozygous]) short pea plant appearing among F_2 plants is one in four, or 25 percent.

To see how *expected results* may be modified by probability, you can use two pennies, one bright and shiny and one tarnished and dull, to represent gametes from two members of the heterozygous F_1 generation (Tt). The heads side of the bright penny represents the dominant factor for tallness (T_1); its tails side represents the factor for shortness (t_1). Similarly, the heads side of the dull penny represents the tallness factor from a second plant (T_2); the tails side represents the factor for shortness (t_2).

Each coin has the same chance of turning up heads as it does tails. Consequently, if the two coins are tossed at the same time, the probability of two heads can be expected in one fourth of the trials. The same is true of two tails. That means a heads matched with a tails can be expected in one half the trials. Figure 3 shows why such outcomes can be expected.

Ask a friend to help you by flipping one of the pennies; you will

23

flip the other. You can both flip the coins at the same time. Let them fall to the floor and then record the results in a data table like the one in Table 3. Use simple check marks like the ones shown in the table to record the result of each toss of the coins.

After 12 tosses, what would you expect the results to be? How many times would you expect both coins to be heads? Both tails? One heads and one tails?

What are the actual results? How do they compare with your prediction?

What are the results after 50 tosses of the two coins? After 100 tosses? After 200 tosses? How does the number of tosses affect the

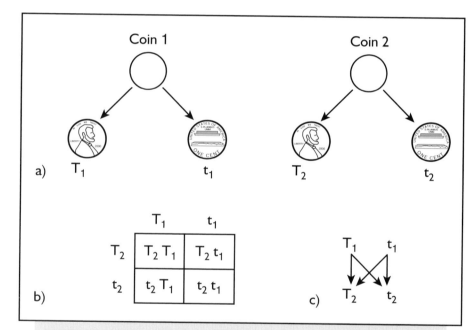

Figure 3. a) Two coins are tossed. Each has an equal probability of landing heads or tails up. b) One way to show the probabilities is to list the possibilities for one coin along a horizontal axis and the possibilities for the other coin along a vertical axis. As you can see, both coins can be expected to land heads up in one fourth of the trials. The same is true for their both landing tails up. One heads and one tails can be expected in half the trials. c) This diagram also shows the possibilities when two coins are tossed simultaneously.

Table 3. A data table for recording the results of tossing two coins at the same time. The results of four hypothetical tosses are shown. The results of your first four tosses may be different.

Both heads (T_1T_2)	√
Both tails (t_1t_2)	√
Dull heads/Bright tails (T_2t_1)	√
Bright heads/Dull tails (T_1t_2)	√

actual results as compared to the expected results? Why do you think Mendel used hundreds of plants in his experiments? How do you think Mendel's knowledge of mathematics was useful to him in conducting his experiments?

Exploring on Your Own

Three coins are tossed at the same time. What is the probability that all three coins will be heads? That all three coins will be tails? What are the other possibilities? What is the probability of each possibility?

Another of Mendel's Experiments

Mendel crossed plants homozygous for green pods with plants homozygous for yellow pods. His results, illustrated in Figure 4, revealed that all members of the F_1 generation had green pods.

When members of the F_1 generation were crossed, the F_2 generation showed a ratio of three plants with green pods for every one plant with yellow pods. Figure 4c shows a Punnett square with the results of crossing purebred plants that had yellow pods with

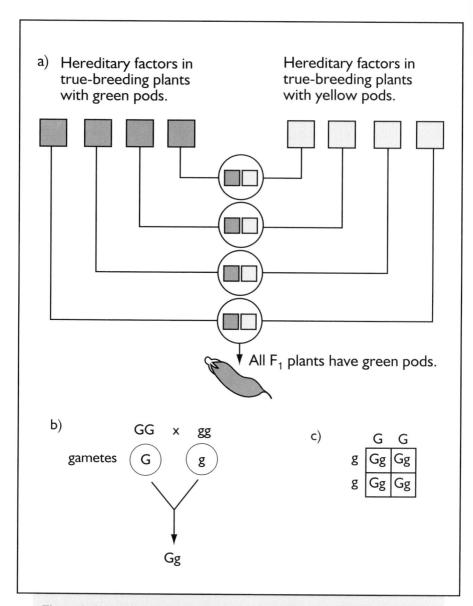

Figure 4. a) A cross between true-breeding pea plants with yellow pods and true-breeding plants with green pods. All the F₁ plants will have green pods. b) The same cross can be represented by symbols. *G* represents the dominant factor for green pods; *g* represents the recessive factor for yellow pods. c) A Punnett square representation of P₁ cross.

purebred plants that had green pods. Make another Punnett square to show the offspring of the F_1 generation.

Mendel wondered what would happen if he examined two pairs of hereditary factors through several generations of pea plants. Would they behave as separate factors or would they stick together?

To find out, he crossed true-breeding tall plants that had green pods with true-breeding short plants that had yellow pods. He found that all the plants in the F_1 generation were tall and bore green pods. The results did not surprise him, because tallness and green pods are both dominant traits.

When he crossed plants from the F_1 generation, he found that $9/16$ of the F_2 plants were tall and had green pods, $3/16$ were tall with yellow pods, $3/16$ were short with green pods, and $1/16$ had both recessive traits. They were short and had yellow pods. This was a ratio of 9:3:3:1.

1-3*
Modeling the Inheritance of Two Independent Traits

Mendel was not surprised by the results of his experiment. Were you? See if you can develop a model to explain the 9:3:3:1 ratio he obtained in the F_2 generation. Remember, in his P_1 generation, plants homozygous for tallness and green pods were crossed with short plants with yellow pods.

Things you will need:

- 48 brown beans and 48 white beans
- 48 dry green split peas and 48 dry yellow split peas
- 4 paper cups
- pen or pencil
- notebook

Now compare your model with Mendel's. Mendel reasoned that hereditary factors are independent of one another and are passed independently to the next generation through the plant's gametes. To see how this works, you can once again represent the factor for tall plants with brown beans and the factor for short plants with white beans. Dry green split peas can be used to represent the dominant factor for green pods. Dry yellow split peas can be used to represent the recessive factor for yellow pods.

From Experiment 1-1, you know that the F_1 generation will be heterozygous (with different inherited factors) for both height (Tt) and pod color (Gg). T represents the factor for tallness, t the factor for shortness. Similarly, G represents the dominant factor for green pods and g the recessive factor for yellow pods. Figure 5 shows the gametes produced by the P_1 plants and the factors found in the F_1 generation, where all the plants are heterozygous for height and pod color.

To make a model of the factors for height and pod color in the F_1 plants, place two dozen dry brown beans and an equal number of dry white beans in a paper cup (Cup 1). Do the same with a second cup (Cup 2). Cover the cups with your hand and shake them to thoroughly mix the seeds. The two kinds of beans represent the hereditary factors for height that can be in a gamete from an F_1 pea plant. The reason for the two cups is that one factor for height comes from each of two parents.

Add two dozen dry green split peas and an equal number of dry yellow split peas to a third paper cup (Cup 3). Do the same with a fourth cup (Cup 4). Cover the cups with your hand and shake them to thoroughly mix the seeds.

Put Cup 1 with beans and Cup 3 with split peas next to one another. Place Cups 2 and 4 close to one another but apart from the

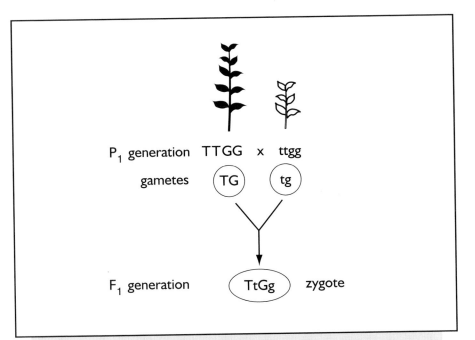

Figure 5. These diagrams show a cross between plants homozygous for tallness (TT) and green pods (GG) with plants homozygous for shortness (tt) and yellow pods (gg). The gametes from one plant carry the factors T and G. The gametes from the other plant carry the factors t and g. The F_1 generation will consist of plants that are tall with green pods. However, they will be heterozygous for these traits (TtGg). What types of gametes will the F_1 generation produce (TtGg X TtGg)?

first two. Pair 1 and 3 and pair 2 and 4 contain the factors for height and pod color present in a parent. The "gametes" from these two parents will be joined to form the seeds of the F_2 generation. Each gamete will contain a hereditary factor for height and pod color.

Close your eyes and reach into a cup that holds the different colored beans. Remove one bean from the cup. Do the same for the cup next to it that contains the two types of split peas. Put these two "hereditary factors" together. They represent the factors for height and pod color that will be in a gamete from one parent. Similarly, join the hereditary factors for height and pod color that will be in a gamete from the second parent. Mendel assumed, as you have, that each seed receives one factor for height and one factor for pod color from each parent, as shown by the Punnett square in Figure 6.

Any organism has both a *phenotype* and a *genotype*. Its phenotype is its appearance, the way it looks. Its genotype is its genetic makeup, the genes it contains. For example, suppose you have a pea plant that inherited factors for tallness and yellow pods from one parent (Tg) and factors for shortness and green pods from the other (tG). The plant's phenotype is tall with green pods. Its genotype with respect to height and pod color is TtGg (heterozygous for tallness and heterozygous for green pods).

Record the phenotype and genotype of the plant that will be produced by the seeds in Experiment 1-3.

Put the beans and peas back in the cups from which they came. Cover the cups and shake them to mix the seeds. Repeat the process 99 more times so that you will have the results of 100 different unions of gametes. Record phenotype and genotype for each trial.

Examine your results carefully. Will any of the seeds grow to become plants that are short with yellow pods? If so, what fraction of the 100 plants will have both these recessive traits? What fraction will be tall and have green pods? What fraction will be tall with yellow pods? What fraction will be short and have green pods? What fraction of the plants are homozygous for tallness? For shortness?

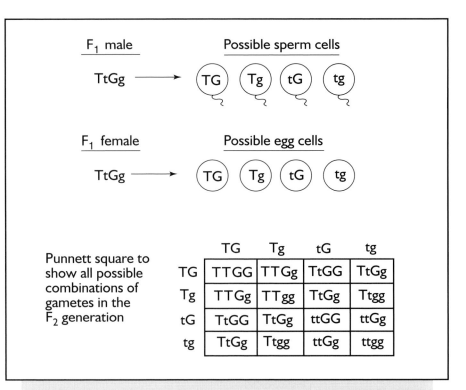

Figure 6. The F$_1$ generation is heterozygous for height and pod color. They can form four types of gametes for these two traits. The Punnett square shows the gametes and the factors in 16 possible seeds that can form when these gametes unite. What fraction of the F$_2$ plants can be expected to be tall with green pods? Tall with yellow pods? Short with green pods? Short with yellow pods?

What fraction of the plants are homozygous for green pods? For yellow pods?

How closely do your results agree with the 9:3:3:1 phenotype ratio that Mendel expected from the cross TtGg X TtGg?

Exploring on Your Own

Develop a model to explain the various offspring that can be expected in the F$_1$ and F$_2$ generations from a P$_1$ cross of plants homozygous for tallness, round seeds, and green pods with plants that are short with wrinkled seeds and yellow pods.

31

Develop a model to explain the various offspring that can be expected in the F_1 and F_2 generations from the P_1 cross of plants homozygous for tallness, round seeds, yellow cotyledons, brown seed coats, and inflated, green, axial pods with plants that are short with wrinkled seeds, green cotyledons, clear seed coats, and constructed, yellow, terminal pods.

2

Mendel, Genes, Chromosomes, and Models

Mendel published the results of his experiments in 1866. His work was ignored. Biologists at that time were engrossed in Darwin's theory of evolution and paid attention to little else. Furthermore, many biologists who did read Mendel's paper were confused by his mathematical analysis of data.

In 1900, Hugo de Vries (1848–1935), a Dutch botanist, rediscovered Mendel's paper. De Vries, who had studied the inherited traits of primroses, was searching the literature for similar studies when he found Mendel's paper. He quickly realized that he had reached the same conclusions as had Mendel.

But de Vries's work went beyond Mendel's. He observed that every once in a while a new variety of primrose that differed significantly from others would suddenly appear and reproduce. De Vries had discovered the underlying cause of evolution. The sudden appearance of new traits were called mutations (from the Latin word *mutare*, meaning "to change"). Experiments demonstrated that a mutation that appeared in one member of a species could be transmitted to its offspring. If the change provided organisms with an adaptation that enabled them to better cope with their environment, then they were more likely to survive than other members of the species. Over time, the accumulation of mutations could lead to a new species. Mendel had discovered the basic manner in which traits are transmitted from generation to generation. De Vries had discovered mutations, the explanation for variation within a species that Darwin had sought.

Chromosomes and Genes

As microscopes improved, biologists began to observe details inside plant and animal cells. Most cells contained a spherical object that came to be known as the nucleus. Surrounding the nucleus was the jellylike cytoplasm. And while the cytoplasm of muscle, nerve, connective, blood, and epithelial cells was quite different, the nuclei of these cells appeared to be similar.

In 1879, Walther Flemming (1843–1905), a German anatomist, found that material within the nuclei of cells readily absorbed a red dye he was using to stain cells. He called this stringlike material chromatin, from the Greek word for color (*chrōma*). By adding the dye to growing tissue, he could examine the chromatin at different stages of cell division. He found that as a cell began to divide, the chromatin became shorter and thicker, forming what came to be known as chromosomes ("colored bodies"). Flemming was able to observe the chromosomes at different stages of cell division, a process he called mitosis.

During the process, the stringlike chromatin winds into short, thick structures called chromosomes. The membrane surrounding the nucleus breaks down, and thin fibers known as spindle fibers form and attach to the chromosomes. As Figure 7 shows, each chromosome replicates (copies itself) so that the number of chromosomes doubles. The duplicates are then separated as they are pulled to opposite sides of the cell; two new cells form, each having the same number of chromosomes as the parent cell.

Biologists who studied mitosis were puzzled. If gametes have the same number of chromosomes as other cells, the zygotes formed by the union of sperm and egg cells would have twice as many chromosomes as their parents. Since all the cells of an organism appeared to come from the repeated mitotic division of the zygote, the number of chromosomes in the cells would double in each successive generation.

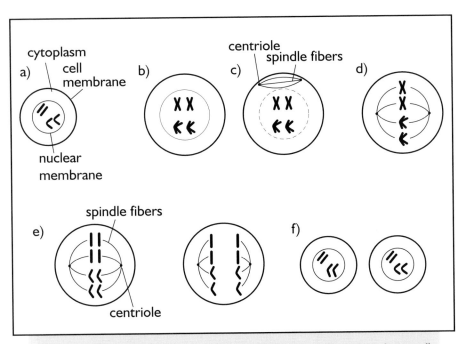

Figure 7. Mitosis is the duplication of chromosomes in a cell's nucleus during cell division. As a result of mitosis, each daughter cell has the same number and type of chromosomes as the parent cell. This diagram shows a cell with two pairs of chromosomes. a) A cell before mitosis. b) Each chromosome replicates. c) The nuclear membrane disappears; spindle fibers form. d) Spindle fibers attach to chromosomes lined up in the center of the cell. e) The chromosomes separate and move to opposite sides of the cell. f) The cell divides, nuclear membranes form, and two daughter cells now exist, each with the same chromosomes as the parent cell.

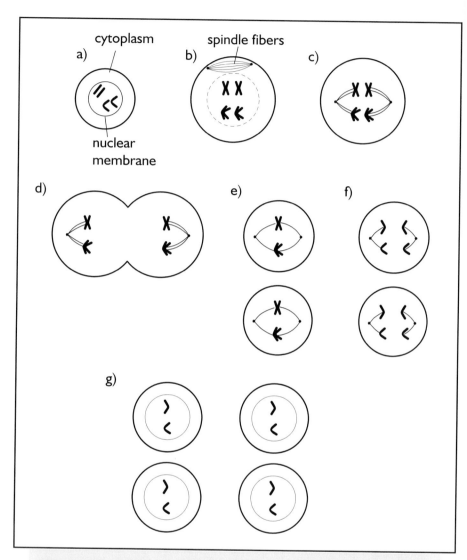

Figure 8. During meiosis each gamete receives only one member of each pair of chromosomes found in other cells of the body. Human cells have 46 chromosomes (23 pairs). Human sperm and egg cells have 23 chromosomes (one from each pair). a) The parent cells that give rise to gametes have the typical number of chromosomes for that species. b) Each chromosome replicates as the nuclear membrane disappears and spindle fibers form. c) The chromosomes line up in matching pairs on the cell's equator. d) One pair of each of the matching pairs of chromosomes goes to opposite sides of the cell. The cell then divides, forming two daughter cells. e) Chromosomes in the daughter cells line up and are attached to spindle fibers. f) Each pair of chromosomes in the daughter cells separates and goes to opposite sides of the cell. g) The cells divide to form four gametes. Each gamete has one member of each pair of chromosomes.

Careful observations of the cell divisions that occur during the formation of gametes provided an answer. Gametes, unlike other cells, are formed by a different type of cell division—a process that came to be known as meiosis, from a Greek word meaning "to diminish." During meiosis, only one member of each pair of chromosomes reaches a sperm or egg cell (see Figure 8). Consequently, the number of chromosomes in the gametes is half the number found in other cells. When gametes unite to form a zygote, the chromosomes pair up again, and the number of chromosomes per cell is restored to the number typical of the species. For humans, that number is 46 (23 pairs).

The discovery of chromosomes provided biologists with the actual matter that could transmit inherited traits from parents to off-spring. The chromosomes were believed to be made up of smaller chemical units, called genes, that were the source of all inherited traits. The factors for the yellow or green color of peas, the height of the pea plants, the color of human eyes, and all other inherited characteristics were transmitted by genes found along the chromosomes in the nuclei of gametes.

2-1*
A Look at Chromosomes

Obtain microscope slides that have been stained to reveal different stages of mitosis and meiosis. The most commonly used cells are from onions,

Things you will need:
- prepared slides of mitosis and meiosis
- microscope

ascarids (roundworms), and whitefish. You may be able to borrow such slides and a microscope from your school's science department. A biology teacher might be willing to show you how to prepare such slides yourself.

Examine slides of mitosis. Can you see cells in which there is a distinct nuclear membrane and strands of chromatin? If you can, you are observing a cell that was not yet undergoing cell division. This step in cell division is called interphase. Cells in which the nuclear membrane disappears and spindle fibers are evident are in prophase. If you see chromosomes lined up near the cell's equator and attached to the spindle fibers, the cell is in metaphase. Can you see spindle fibers during metaphase? Can you detect cells where the chromosomes are separating and being pulled to opposite sides of the cell? These cells are in anaphase. In the last phase of cell division, known as telophase, the chromosomes are clustered at opposite sides of a cell and a new cell membrane is forming between them. The result is two daughter cells. What differences would you expect to find between cells undergoing mitosis as compared with those undergoing meiosis? Can you detect any such differences?

Exploring on Your Own

Investigate how you might use an onion root tip to prepare a slide that would reveal various stages of cells undergoing mitosis. Then examine these slides under a microscope.

Investigate how you might use an anther from a lily flower to prepare a slide that would reveal various stages of cells undergoing meiosis. Then examine these slides under a microscope.

2-2*
A Model of Mitosis

Things you will need:

- 12 white pipe cleaners or twisties
- colored felt-tip pen
- paper

A physical model is helpful in understanding what happens to chromosomes during mitosis. You can use pipe cleaners or twisties to represent chromosomes. On a sheet of paper, draw a large circle to represent a cell. Prepare four (two pairs of) model chromosomes, as shown in Figure 9a. Bend the tips of one pair. Color one member of each pair with a felt-tip pen so that you can distinguish it from its twin.

Line up the "chromosomes," one after the other, along the equator of the cell you drew on paper. These figures represent the metaphase part of mitosis, as shown in Figure 9b. At this point the

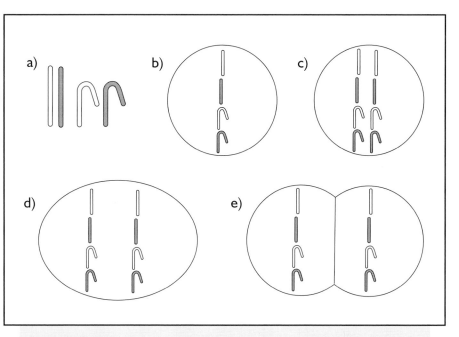

Figure 9. Pipe cleaners or twisties can be used to model chromosomes in the process of mitosis.

chromosomes replicate. Consequently, use pipe cleaners and a colored felt-tip pen to prepare four more chromosomes identical to the first four. Place them next to their identical partners, as shown in Figure 9c. Next, separate the identical chromosomes as occurs during the anaphase part of mitosis (Figure 9d). Finally (Figure 9e), draw a line between the separated chromosomes to show that cell division has occurred.

How does the number of chromosomes in the two new cells compare with the number that were in the original cell? How does the number of pairs of chromosomes in the two new cells compare with the number that were in the original cell?

If these pipe cleaners or twisties represent the number of chromosomes characteristic of a particular species, how many pairs of chromosomes are in each body cell of a member of this species? How many chromosomes will be found in the gametes produced by

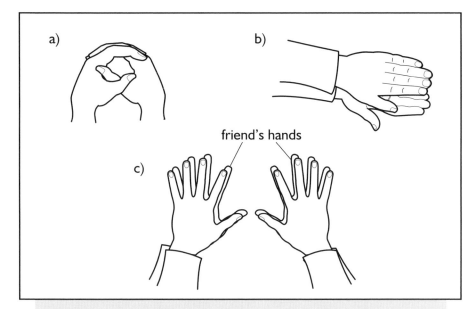

Figure 10. A model of mitosis using fingers to represent chromosomes. a) The cell in prophase. b) The cell in metaphase before replication of chromosomes. c) The cell in metaphase after replication.

this species? How many members of each pair of chromosomes will be in the gametes of this species?

Another Model of Mitosis

Here is another simple model of mitosis involving five pairs of "chromosomes." Let the fingers on your two hands represent five pairs of chromosomes. If you fold your hands together as shown in Figure 10a, your fingers represent the chromosomes wound up inside the nucleus as they are normally during prophase. Now place one hand above the other with fingers extended (Figure 10b). Your fingers now represent the chromosomes as they line up in the center of the cell during mitosis. Have a friend place his or her hands against yours to represent the chromosomes after they have duplicated themselves during metaphase (Figure 10c). How can you continue this model to show anaphase, telophase, and two new cells in interphase?

In this model, how does the number of chromosomes in the two new cells compare with the number in the original cell?

Exploring on Your Own

What is a centromere and where is it found?

What are telomeres? How may they be related to an organism's natural life span?

2-3*
A Model of Meiosis

A physical model is even more helpful in understanding what happens to chromosomes during meiosis when sperm or egg cells are produced. Pipe cleaners or twisties can, again, represent chromosomes, but you will need twice as many as before. Prepare

four (two pairs of) model chromosomes. Do this twice so that you have a total of eight chromosomes, as shown in Figure 11a.

Attach a small piece of green yarn to one member of each pair of the straight chromosomes. The yarn will represent the gene for green pod color. To the mate in each pair, at a corresponding place, attach a small piece of yellow yarn to represent the gene for yellow pod color.

To one member of each pair of the hook-shaped chromosomes, attach a long piece of dark yarn to represent the gene for tallness. To its mate in each pair, at a corresponding place, attach a short piece of dark yarn to represent the gene for shortness.

These are the "genes" and "chromosomes" that would be present in the F_1 generation following a cross of pea plants homozygous for green pods and tallness with short plants that produce yellow pods.

On a sheet of paper, draw two large circles to represent two cells. Line up the chromosomes in pairs along the equator of each cell to represent the metaphase part of meiosis. (Remember, in meiosis the chromosomes are paired during metaphase.) As you can see from Figures 11b and 11b´, the two pairs of chromosomes can line up in two different ways. The straight chromosome with the gene for green pods can be on the same side of the equator as the

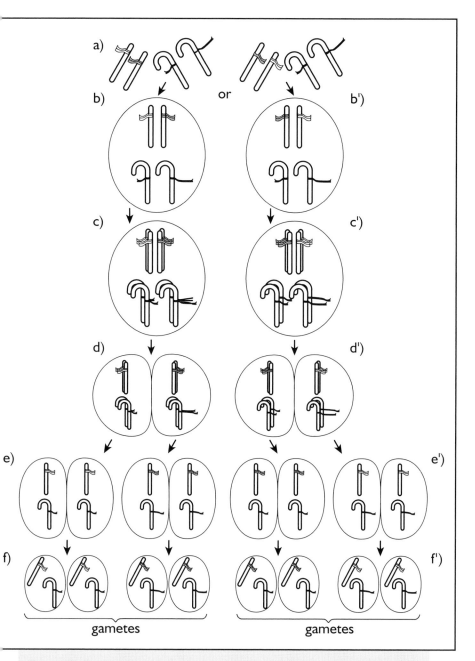

Figure 11. During meiosis one member of each pair of chromosomes enters each gamete. This is accomplished by two cell divisions. Only during the first cell division do the chromosomes replicate.

hook-shaped chromosome carrying the gene for shortness, or on the same side as the one that carries the gene for tallness.

During the metaphase of meiosis, the chromosomes replicate themselves, forming four-chromosome clusters (known as tetrads) around the equator of the cell. Use pipe cleaners or twisties and colored yarn to prepare eight more chromosomes identical to the first eight. Place them next to their identical partners, as shown in Figure 11c and 11c′. Next, separate the identical chromosomes as happens during the anaphase part of the first meiotic cell division (Figure 11d and 11d′). Draw a line between the separated chromosomes to show that the cell has divided.

If cell division stopped here, how many chromosomes would be in the gametes (sperm or egg cells)? How many chromosomes would be in the zygote formed by the union of sperm and egg cells? What would happen to the number of chromosomes in the cells of the organism in each succeeding generation?

The second cell division in meiosis reduces the chromosome number to half the number found in the other cells of the organism. To see how this happens, separate the chromosomes you have in each cell after the first cell division (Figure 11d and 11d′). Move them to opposite sides of a cell nucleus and draw a line to represent cell division, as shown in Figure 11e and 11e′. This represents the second meiotic division. Finally, place the chromosomes in cells that have separated into four distinct "gametes," as shown in Figure 11f and 11f′.

How does the number of chromosomes in the gametes compare with the number that were in the original parent cell prior to meiosis? How many members of each pair of chromosomes are in each of the gametes? How many distinct types of gametes are there? How many would there be in a species that has four pairs of chromosomes? Humans have 23 pairs of chromosomes. How many chromosomes would you expect to find in human egg or sperm cells?

Exploring on Your Own

Use your hands and those of a friend to make a model of chromosomes during the two cell divisions that constitute meiosis.

Pea plants that are homozygous tall with yellow pods are crossed with short pea plants that are homozygous for green pods. Use a chromosome model to show that in the F_2 generation you can expect to find plants in a ratio of 9 tall with green pods:3 tall with yellow pods:3 short with green pods:1 short with yellow pods.

Use chromosome models to show that the traits Mendel studied—height, seed shape, color of the seed leaves, seed coats, pod shape, pod color, and position of pods on the stem—must have been located on different chromosomes.

Is there any evidence to suggest that it may be possible to make artificial chromosomes? If it were to become possible, would it offer any benefits to humans?

Fruit Flies (Drosophila melanogaster)

Early in the twentieth century, a number of geneticists began experimenting with a species of fruit flies called *Drosophila melanogaster*. This fruit fly was ideal for genetic studies. It was easy to raise, reproduced rapidly, and possessed a number of inherited traits that could be readily identified. Furthermore, each female produced many fertile eggs. Because the species produced so many offspring, the results were mathematically meaningful. In fact, the flies reproduced in such abundance that experimenters would occasionally see a mutant fly. For example, once in a while a fly with white or ebony eyes would appear instead of the red-eyed type seen normally. One scientist, Hermann Joseph Muller (1890–1967), found that he could increase the rate of mutation by subjecting the flies or their eggs to X rays. It was Muller who realized that X rays, which had only recently been discovered by Wilhelm Conrad Röntgen (1845–1923), are dangerous because they can change genes.

To become more familiar with this animal, so commonly used in genetics, you might like to use it in some experiments. Through your school, you can buy *D. melanogaster* and the supplies needed to grow and experiment with them from almost any science supply house that sells biological materials.

Like most insects, these flies have a life cycle that includes eggs, larvae, pupae, and adult stages. The entire life cycle takes only 10–14 days, depending on temperature. Changes occur faster in a warm room than in a cool one. The adult females lay eggs about 36 hours after mating. The eggs hatch into larvae after about a day. The larvae then begin to feed on the medium provided. When geneticists first began to experiment with fruit flies, they used ripe bananas as a medium, but most laboratories today use a prepared medium that usually contains agar, cornmeal, corn syrup, molasses, water, and a mold retardant.

2-4*
Experimenting with Drosophila melanogaster

Genetic experiments with *Drosophila melanogaster* are not difficult to carry out. However, they do require some training, and they may involve the use of a chemical (ethyl ether) that can be hazardous. For those reasons, you should carry out genetic experiments **under the supervision of a knowledgeable adult**, such as a science teacher or biologist who has had experience with fruit flies.

To gain experience in making genetic crosses with these flies, ask the adult to help you mate male and female fruit flies that are both of the wild type (normal). You can then watch the entire life cycle over the next 10–14 days. One thing you will have to learn is how to distinguish between male and female flies. Figure 12 may help, but hands-on separation of the sexes under adult supervision is essential. In the figure, the circle with an arrow extending from it (♂) is the symbol for male. The circle with the cross beneath it (♀) is the symbol for female.

After developing some technique in managing fruit fly crosses, you can, **under adult supervision**, begin some experiments in which you mate wild-type flies with flies that have a variety of different traits. Of course, since they mate only once, it is essential that you know how to isolate young flies that have not mated prior to

Things you will need:
- knowledgeable adult
- medium and containers for growing flies (most science supply houses will provide media, necessary supplies, and flies, along with instructions)
- a means of anesthetizing the flies, such as ether
- glass plate on which to examine the flies
- magnifying glass
- watercolor paint brush to separate flies
- morgue (baby food jar with motor oil or alcohol)
- cultures of wild-type flies
- cultures of experimental flies (flies with genes not common in wild-type flies)

the experiment you wish to conduct. Your instructor can show you how to do this. Some of the experiments you might try are listed below. The letter X represents the word *cross*, which means "to mate."

- Wild-type (winged) flies X wingless flies, followed by an F_1 cross of the resulting offspring.

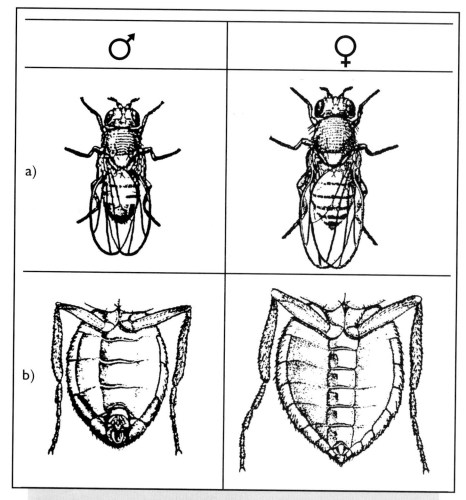

Figure 12. a) A magnified view of a male and female fruit fly from above. b) A magnified view of the underside of the abdomen of a male and female fruit fly.

- Wild-type (red-eyed) males X sepia- (brown-) eyed females, followed by an F_1 cross of the resulting offspring.

- Vestigial-winged, red-eyed flies X normal-winged, sepia-eyed flies, followed by an F_1 cross of the resulting offspring.

- White-eyed females X red-eyed males, followed by an F_1 cross of the resulting offspring.

Exploring on Your Own

Under adult supervision, develop your own variety of fruit fly cultures and prepare your own media. Invite others, also **under adult supervision**, who are interested in genetics to experiment with the flies and share their results with you.

Are there any results that you cannot explain?

3

Heredity and Family

Understanding human genetics is fascinating but often difficult. Many human traits are inherited, but they cannot be investigated experimentally. Geneticists cannot require a man with curly black hair and green eyes to marry a woman who has straight red hair and brown eyes. These scientists must look for people with particular characteristics who have married and had children. Furthermore, people often dye their hair, even change their eye color, so that their natural traits may be hidden. In addition, humans have relatively few offspring; most human characteristics are the result of more than one pair of genes; and many traits, such as height and weight, are affected by environmental factors. For example, even though a person possesses genes for normal size, he or she may be short and frail because of poor nutrition. Much of what geneticists know about human inheritance comes from interviewing people and drawing a family tree (a pedigree) to try to figure out how a trait is inherited.

A Family Tree

In drawing a family tree, females are represented by circles, males by squares. A horizontal line connecting a circle and a square

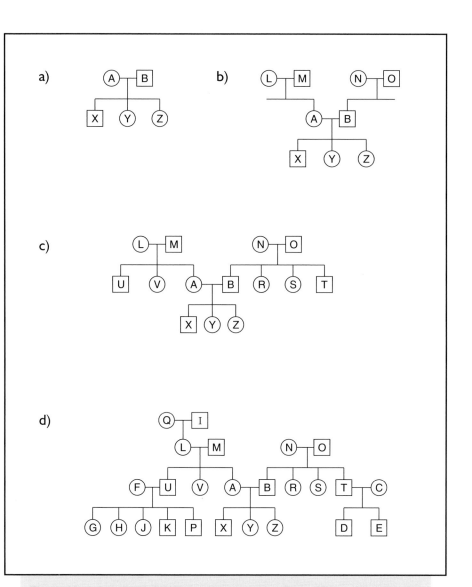

Figure 13. a) A pedigree (family tree) showing the offspring from a marriage of A and B. Squares represent males; circles represent females. b) Branches have been added to show the parents of A and B (the grandparents of X, Y, and Z). c) The sibling lines have been extended to show the brothers and sisters of A and B. d) The children of siblings U and T have been added. The parents of L (Q and I, who are the grandparents of A and great-grandparents of X, Y, and Z) have also been added.

represents a marriage. It can be called a marriage line. A short vertical line leading downward from the marriage line connects to a second horizontal line. This line has short vertical lines beneath it that lead to the circles and squares representing their children.

Figure 13a shows two married people, A and B, and their children X, Y, and Z. Figure 13b shows that A and B were the children of parents L and M, N and O, who are the grandparents of X, Y, and Z. Figure 13c reveals that these grandparents had other children—U and V and R, S, and T. U and V are A's siblings; R, S, and T are B's siblings. In Figure 13d, we learn that A's brother, U, married F, and they had five children, G, H, J, K, and P. B's brother, T, married C, and they had two children, D and E. We also discover that L was the only child of Q and I.

Notice that all members of the same generation are placed on the same horizontal level. This makes it easy to see that X, Y, and Z are the first cousins of G, H, J, K, and P, as well as D and E.

Once you have drawn as much of a family's pedigree as possible, you can begin to look for traits that have been transmitted from one generation to the next. If a person on the family tree is dead or

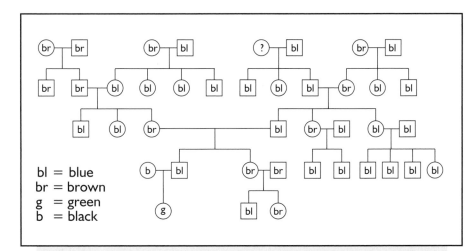

bl = blue
br = brown
g = green
b = black

Figure 14. A pedigree of a family that shows the eye color of most members of the family.

living too far away to be observed, you will have to rely on his or her descendants to provide information about that person's phenotype. For example, the author's family tree, shown in Figure 14, can be used to trace eye color. A key is provided so that individuals and their eye color can be identified quickly.

In some instances, the genetics of a trait is well understood. In those cases, the genotype or genotype possibilities of a family member can be determined by knowing the phenotypes of his or her closest relatives. For example, Huntington's disease (HD), a severe debilitating affliction that attacks people after age 30, is known to be carried by a rare dominant gene. If someone has the disease, he

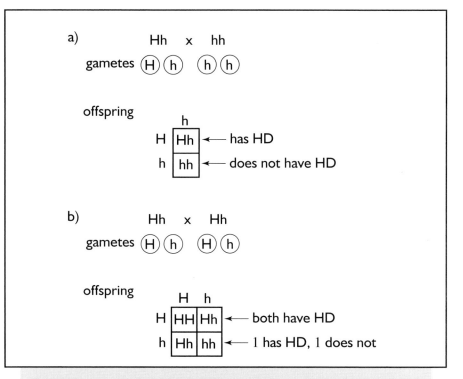

Figure 15. a) Huntington's disease (HD) is carried by a rare dominant gene, H. If one parent has the gene, he or she will be affected and their children will have a 50:50 chance of inheriting the disease. b) If both parents have HD, the chances are 3:1 that the offspring will inherit the disease.

or she is most likely heterozygous because the gene is rare. His or her offspring stand a 50:50 chance of inheriting the disorder because they have an equal chance of receiving either the dominant or the recessive gene from the affected parent. The parent without the disease will transmit only the recessive gene. See Figure 15a. In the highly unlikely case that both parents have the disease, their offspring's chances of inheriting the disorder are 3:1 (see Figure 15b).

3-1
Tracing an Inherited Trait

Look again at the pedigree of a family for eye color, shown below (previously Figure 14). If both parents in this pedigree are blue-eyed, what is the color of their children's eyes? If both

Things you will need:
- paper, preferably lined or graph paper
- pencil
- Figure 14

parents have brown eyes, do all their children have brown eyes? Based on this family alone, why might you conclude that the gene for brown eyes is dominant to the gene for blue eyes? Assuming eye color is controlled by a single pair of genes—one for blue eyes and one for brown—make a copy of the family tree showing the genotype of each person. Does the assumption hold for everyone in the family tree?

Does the gene for eye color appear to depend on whether the individual is male or female? What evidence do you have to support your answer?

What evidence is there in this family tree to indicate that more than one pair of genes (blue or brown) is involved in determining eye color?

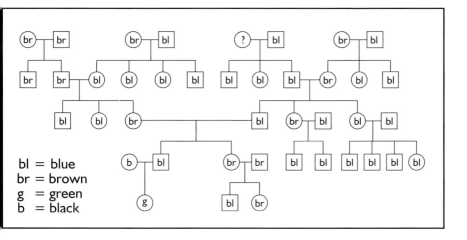

bl = blue
br = brown
g = green
b = black

55

3-2*
Making Your Own Family Tree

To make your family tree, use lined paper and a pencil, because you will probably have to redraw the tree at least once. Draw the symbol that represents you (a square or a circle) near

Things you will need:

- paper, preferably lined or graph paper
- pencil
- family members

the center of the paper. Put your initials inside. Add your siblings if you have any, and write their initials inside the squares or circles. Add a vertical line upward to another horizontal line that connects your parents. On the same level as your parents, add your aunts and uncles and, if they are married, the people to whom they are married. Their children (your cousins) should be on the same level as you and your siblings. Where should you place your grandparents on this family tree? How about your great-grandparents? Is there enough information (ask your parents) to add your great-great-grandparents to the family tree? How about your great-great-great-grandparents? How many people have you placed on your family tree?

Keep the family tree you have made. It will be useful in the experiments that follow.

Exploring on Your Own

Make additions to your family tree as new people join your family through marriage or birth. If you keep it long enough, you can add your own children and your nieces and nephews to the tree.

If small photographs are available, you could make an enlarged family tree with photographs in place of circles and squares.

3-3
Tracing Eye Color in Your Family

Use the family tree you made in Experiment 3-2. With colored pencils, mark the lower right-hand corner or section of each square or circle with a color to match the eye color of each fam-

Things you will need:

• family tree from Experiment 3-2

• colored pencils

• family members

ily member. How do the results for your family compare with those found for the family in Experiment 3-1?

3-4
Taste, PTC, and Genetics

About 70 percent of the American population can taste a chemical commonly known as PTC (phenylthiocarbamide). A solution of the chemical can be used to saturate paper strips that can be dried and preserved. When some people chew a strip of PTC paper, they sense a definite taste.

Things you will need:

- phenylthiocarbamide (PTC) paper strips (available from school biology department or from a science supply house)
- as many related people as possible from your family and other families
- pen or pencil
- notebook

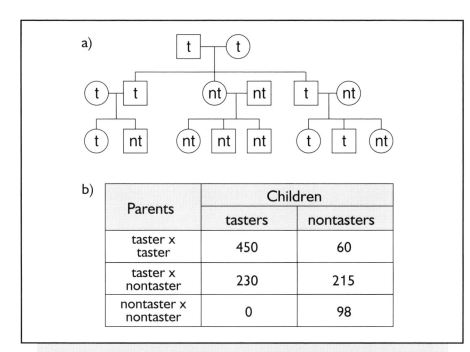

Figure 16. In the family history shown in (a), tasters (people who can taste PTC) are represented by a *t*; nontasters are represented by *nt*. The data table provided in (b) is from a study of many families. Based on the data provided, do you think the ability to taste PTC is transmitted by a dominant or by a recessive gene? Why?

Place a strip of PTC paper in your mouth and chew it. Discard the paper after you have chewed it for a short time. Are you a taster or a nontaster? If you are a taster, describe the taste of PTC. Does it taste sweet, sour, bitter, or salty? If you are a nontaster, ask other people to chew a strip of the paper until you find a taster. How does a taster describe the taste of PTC?

Continue to test as many people as possible from different generations of your family and other families. Record your results and be sure to indicate the relationship among the people you test. Based on all the data you have collected, prepare family trees to show how the gene is transmitted through generations. Based on the pedigree, can you decide whether the ability to taste PTC is the result of a dominant or a recessive gene?

If you obtained results like those shown in Figure 16a, what might you conclude about the gene that transmits the ability to taste PTC? Would you change your mind on the basis of the data provided by the table in Figure 16b?

3-5
Taste, Thiourea, and Genetics

Another chemical that some people can taste and others cannot is thiourea. Place a strip of thiourea paper in your mouth and chew it. Discard the paper after you have chewed it for a short time. Are you a taster or a nontaster? If you are a taster, describe the taste of thiourea. Does it taste sweet, sour, bitter, or salty? If you are a nontaster,

Things you will need:

• thiourea paper strips (available from school biology department or from a science supply house)

• as many related people as possible from your family and other families

• pen or pencil

• notebook

ask other people to chew a strip of the paper until you find a taster. How does a taster describe the taste of thiourea?

Continue to test as many people as possible from different generations of your family and other families. Record your results and be sure to indicate the relationship among the people you test. Based on all the data you have collected, can you decide whether the ability to taste thiourea is the result of a dominant or a recessive gene?

3-6
Taste, Sodium Benzoate, and Genetics

Still another chemical that some people can taste and others cannot is sodium benzoate. Place a strip of sodium benzoate paper in your mouth and chew it. Discard the paper after you have chewed it for a short time. Are you a taster or a nontaster? If you are a taster, describe the taste of sodium benzoate. Does it taste sweet, sour, bitter, or

Things you will need:

• sodium benzoate paper strips (available from school biology department or from a science supply house)

• as many related people as possible from your family and other families

• pen or pencil

• notebook

salty? If you are a nontaster, ask other people to chew a strip of the paper until you find a taster. How does a taster describe the taste of sodium benzoate?

Continue to test as many people as possible from different generations of your family and other families. Record your results and be sure to indicate the relationship among the people you test. Based on family trees made from all the data you have collected, can you decide whether the ability to taste sodium benzoate is the result of a dominant or a recessive gene?

3-7
The Inheritance of Other Human Traits

Cleft Chin

Cleft chin (see Figure 17a) is believed to be the result of a dominant gene. Collect data from your own and/or other families where some family members have a cleft chin. Do your data support the idea that cleft chin is caused by a dominant gene? If not, what does it indicate?

Things you will need:

* as many related people as possible from your family and other families

* pen or pencil

* notebook

Dimples

Dimples (see Figure 17b), too, are believed to be the result of a dominant gene. Collect data from your own and/or other families where some of the people have dimples. Do your data support the idea that dimples are caused by a dominant gene? If not, what does it indicate?

Rolled Tongue

The ability to roll your tongue lengthwise (see Figure 17c) is believed to be the result of yet another dominant gene. Collect data from your own and/or other families where some family members are able to roll their tongues. Do your data support the idea that this ability is the result of a dominant gene? If not, what does it indicate?

Earlobes

Earlobes can be free or attached (see Figure 17d). Collect data from your own and/or other families where some family members have free earlobes and others have attached earlobes. Does either trait appear to be the result of a dominant gene? If not, what, if anything, do your data indicate about the inheritance of this trait?

Thumb Shape

As shown in Figure 17e, extended thumbs can be straight or curved. Collect data from your own and/or other families where some of the people have straight thumbs and others have curved thumbs. Does either trait appear to be the result of a dominant gene? If not, what, if anything, do your data indicate about the inheritance of this trait?

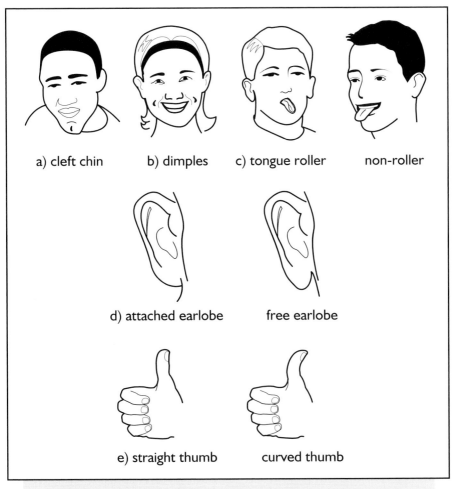

a) cleft chin   b) dimples   c) tongue roller   non-roller

d) attached earlobe   free earlobe

e) straight thumb   curved thumb

Figure 17. A number of readily visible characteristics are inherited.

3-8
Eye Color and Genes

You may have read or heard that eye color is inherited and that the gene for brown eyes is dominant to the gene for blue eyes. Show that if this were true, the following statements are also true. Two blue-eyed parents

Things you will need:

• as many related people as possible from your family and other families

• pen or pencil

• notebook

could have only blue-eyed children. If one or both parents were homozygous for brown eyes (had only the dominant genes for brown eyes), all their children would have brown eyes. If both parents were heterozygous for brown eyes (had a gene for brown and a gene for blue eyes), the chances are that one fourth of their children will have blue eyes and three-fourths will have brown eyes.

Collect evidence to show that such a simple explanation of eye color does not agree with observations of eye color in different people.

Would a gene for dark eyes (black, brown, hazel) dominant to a gene for less-pigmented eyes (blue, green, or gray) be a more satisfactory explanation for the inheritance of eye color?

Suppose eye color is affected by two pairs of genes. If all four genes in these two pairs are dominant genes, we can represent them by the capital letters EE and CC and assume that such a combination (EECC) causes very dark eyes. We can also use small letters, ee and cc, to represent the recessive genes for the same two pairs. If someone has all four recessive genes (eecc), we will assume the person has blue eyes. Someone who is heterozygous for eye color in both pairs (EeCc) might have green eyes or light brown eyes.

Do two pairs of genes affecting eye color provide a better explanation for the inheritance of eye color? Would three pairs of genes provide a better explanation? Collect data to support your answer.

3-9
The Inheritance of Hair Color

Hair comes in many colors— blond, brown, red, chestnut, and black, to name a few. Because of the variation in hair color, it seems likely that it is the result of several pairs of genes. Yet red hair is so distinct that its presence suggests it is a trait controlled by a single gene.

Things you will need:

- as many related people as possible from your family and other families
- pen or pencil
- notebook

Collect as much evidence as you can about hair color by studying your own and other families. Be sure the hair you observe is natural and not altered by dyes or aging (gray hair). Can you draw any conclusions about the inheritance of hair color? If so, what are they?

Human Blood Types

Human blood is of different types. Red blood cells may carry a substance called an antigen. Antigens, known as A and B, are chemical compounds that, when present, cause antibodies to form. These antibodies, known as anti-A and anti-B, react with a specific antigen. The anti-A antibody reacts with the A antigen; the anti-B antibody reacts with the B antigen.

An individual's red blood cells may contain one, both, or neither of the two antigens. Human blood, therefore, can be one of four types: A, B, AB, or O. As you can see from Table 4, a person with type A blood has the A antigen on his or her red blood cells; a person with type B blood has the B antigen; someone with type AB blood has both antigens; and a person with type O blood has neither antigen. Blood serum (the fluid part of blood that remains after blood clots) may contain antibodies that react with the A or B antigens, causing the blood cells to clump together (agglutinate). Agglutination can be seen through a microscope. Consequently, a person's blood type can be readily determined.

As you can see from Table 4, a person with type AB blood has neither antibody. If she did, her antibodies would react with the antigens on her own red blood cells, causing agglutination. Agglutinated cells would be unable to flow through small blood vessels and the person would die.

To determine a person's blood type, a small amount of his or her blood is placed on each of two glass slides. A drop of blood serum containing the anti-A antibody is added to one drop; a drop of serum containing the anti-B antibody is added to the other drop. As Table 5 reveals, either anti-A or anti-B will cause type AB blood to clump. On the other hand, a person with type O blood carries both antibodies but neither antigen on his red blood cells. Therefore, his blood cells will not clump when blood serum with either antibody is added. Someone with type A blood has the A antigen and the anti-B antibodies. Her red blood cells will clump when anti-A serum is added but not when anti-B serum is added. Type B blood, which contains the B antigen, will clump when anti-B serum is added but not when anti-A serum is added.

The percentages of white and black people in the United States with each of the four blood types are found in Table 6. As you can see, type O is the most common, type AB the most rare, and the frequency of each type is related to race.

In addition to the A, B, AB, and O blood types, humans possess

Table 4. The four blood types and the antigens on their red blood cells (RBC) and the antibodies in their blood serum.

Blood type	Antigens on RBC	Antibodies in serum
A	A	Anti-B
B	B	Anti-A
AB	A and B	Neither antibody
O	Neither antigen	Anti-A and Anti-B

Table 5. Typing blood by adding a known antiserum to the blood in question. A plus sign (+) indicates agglutination; a minus sign (–) indicates no agglutination.

Anti-A serum added to the blood sample	Anti-B serum added to the blood sample	Test indicates antigen on the RBC is	Test indicates blood is type
+	–	A	A
–	+	B	B
+	+	A and B	AB
–	–	neither	O

other blood antigens for which tests have been developed. For example, people may be either Rh positive (85%) or Rh negative (15%); they may be type M, type N, or type MN.

Considering all the possible combinations of blood types and enzymes, an individual may be quite unique. For example, the probability of having both type AB and Rh negative blood is 0.04 x 0.15 = 0.006 or 6 people in a thousand. If other blood factors are considered, the probability of finding someone with identical blood may be extremely small.

Table 6. The four blood types and the frequency of their occurrence in two races of Americans.

Blood type	American Whites (%)	American Blacks (%)
O	45	49
A	40	27
B	11	20
AB	4	4

3-10*
Inheritance of Human Blood Types

Because blood tests are so common, most people know their blood type. Someone who tells you he is O-negative has blood that is type O and Rh negative. Obtain the blood types of as many people who are related to

Things you will need:

• as many related people as possible from your family and other families

• pen or pencil

• notebook

one another as possible. Start with your own family. What is your blood type? What are the blood types of your brothers and sisters? What are or were your parents' blood types? Your grandparents? Your great-grandparents? Record all your data. It should include the blood type (O, A, B, or AB; and Rh positive or negative) of each person and the relationships of the people involved.

Then investigate the blood types of other people who are related. Record all that data as well.

One investigation might provide data like that found in the family tree shown in Figure 18. What if anything can you conclude about the inheritance of blood type from the evidence in the table? Does any of the data in Figure 18 conflict with yours?

Geneticists who have studied the inheritance of blood types among humans have found that if both parents are Rh negative, all their children will be Rh negative. In some marriages where both parents are Rh positive, all the children are Rh positive. In other such marriages, some of their offspring are Rh negative. In some marriages where one parent is Rh positive and the other Rh negative, all the children are Rh positive. In other such marriages, some of the children are Rh positive and some are Rh negative. All this suggests that the gene for Rh positive blood is dominant to the gene for Rh negative blood.

Other genetic studies reveal that if both parents have type O blood, all their children will have type O blood. Similarly, in some

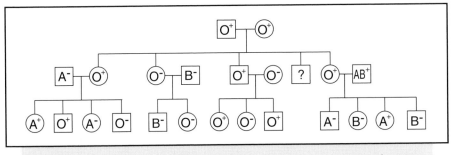

Figure 18. A family tree showing blood types—A, B, AB, and O; and Rh$^+$ or Rh$^-$.

marriages where one parent has type A blood and the other has type O, all the children will have type A blood. In other such marriages, some children will have type A blood and some will have type O.

In some marriages where one parent has type B blood and the other has type O blood, all the children will have type B blood. In

Table 7. The inheritance of A, B, AB, and O blood types based on results from a large group of families.

Blood type of parents	Blood types that may appear in children	Blood types that will not appear in children
O x O	O	A, B, AB
O x A	O, A	B, AB
O x B	O, B	A, AB
O x AB	A, B	O, AB
A x A	A, O	B, AB
A x B	O, A, B, AB	—
A x AB	A, B, AB	O
B x B	O, B	A, AB
B x AB	A, B, AB	O
AB x AB	A, B, AB	O

other such marriages, some children will have type B blood and some will have type O blood.

If a person with type AB blood marries a person with type O blood, their children will have either type A or type B blood. Table 7 summarizes the inheritance of A, B, AB, and O blood types. Do your data agree with the data in the table? Based on all the available data, see if you can explain how these blood types are inherited.

Exploring on Your Own

Blood or bloodstains are often found at crime scenes. Usually the blood type can be determined readily. How might the blood type be used to show that a person suspected of the crime is innocent? Can it be used to prove a person is guilty?

4

Genes That Are Linked

Every living thing has thousands of traits that are passed from one generation to the next. Yet most organisms have relatively few chromosomes. Humans have 23 pairs, corn plants have 10 pairs, fruit flies have only 4 pairs, but crayfish have 104 pairs. If a species' thousands of characteristics are transmitted by the genes that constitute its relatively few chromosomes, many genes must be located on the same chromosome.

Mendel studied just seven characteristics of pea plants, but there are many more—color of the flowers, shape of the leaves, time to mature, and so on. A careful look at the nuclei of pea plants reveals that there are just seven pairs of chromosomes. Apparently, Mendel selected for study seven traits that were all on different chromosomes and, consequently, behaved independently of one another.

Linked Genes

Because the fruit fly has only four pairs of chromosomes, its traits must be inherited in groups of genes that are on the same chromosome. Geneticists soon found that the fruit fly's inherited traits tended to stick in certain patterns as they passed from parents to offspring. We can see such a pattern in the following example of breeding.

Most fruit flies have a gray body. However, there is a recessive mutant gene that, when homozygous (having two identical genes), causes flies to have a black body. Crosses between true breeding gray (GG) and black flies (gg) produce F_1 offspring that are all gray. Crosses of F_1 individuals (genotype Gg) result in a 3:1 gray-to-black ratio, showing that the gene for gray is dominant to the gene for black. There is also a gene, N, for normal-length wings that is dominant to a recessive gene, n, for vestigial (short, stumpy) wings. Flies

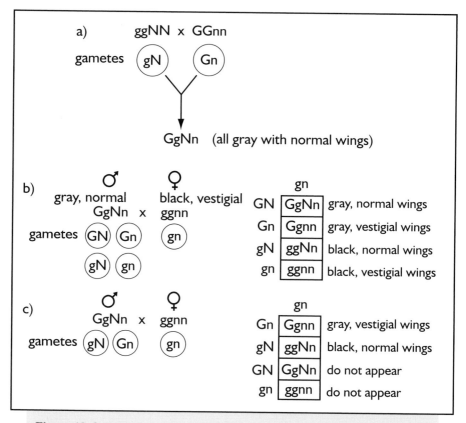

Figure 19. Some genes are linked; they stick together because they are on the same chromosome.

with NN or Nn genotypes have normal wings; those that are homozygous recessive, nn, have vestigial wings.

When flies homozygous for black bodies and normal wings (ggNN) are crossed with flies homozygous for gray bodies and vestigial wings (GGnn), all the offspring will be heterozygous (different genes) for gray bodies and normal wings (GgNn), as shown in Figure 19a.

Now these male flies are crossed with female flies homozygous for black bodies and vestigial wings. If the genes assort independently, we would expect offspring in the ratio of 1 gray body with normal wings:1 gray body with vestigial wings:1 black body with normal wings:1 black body with vestigial wings, as illustrated in Figure 19b.

In fact, we find that half the offspring are gray-bodied with vestigial wings and half are black-bodied with normal wings. How can this be explained?

From Figures 19b and c, it is evident that no gametes (sperm cells) of the GN or gn type are produced by the gray-bodied, normal-winged male parent. Only gametes carrying the gN or Gn gene combination are produced by this heterozygous male. The gN and Gn gametes are the ones that were in the original cross (Figure 19a). The genes g and N came into the cross together, and they stayed together when gametes were formed. They did not assort at random. The same is true of the G and n genes. If genes g and N were on the same chromosome, we would expect them to stay together. Similarly, if G and n were on the same chromosome, we would expect them to stick together.

4-1
A Model for Linked Genes

For the sake of simplicity in this experiment, we will assume that eye color is governed by a single pair of genes. We will let B represent the gene for brown

Things you will need:
• pipe cleaners or twisties
• small pieces of colored yarn

eyes and b the gene for blue eyes. We will also assume that if both genes are present on the pair of chromosomes that carry the genes for eye color, neither gene is dominant and the person will have gray eyes.

We will also assume that hair color is controlled by a single pair of genes. We will let D represent the gene for dark hair and L the gene for light hair. If both genes are present, we will assume the person will have light brown hair.

Finally, we will assume that the genes for hair and eye color are on the same chromosome; that is, they are linked. Figure 20 shows the genes on the pair of chromosomes responsible for hair and eye color for a person who has gray eyes and light brown hair.

Assume that a man who has gray eyes and light brown hair marries a woman who has the same traits. Using pipe cleaners or twisties to represent chromosomes and small pieces of colored yarn to represent genes, prepare models of the "chromosomes" found in the cells of these two people. Assume that the man has the chromosomes shown in Figure 20a and the woman has the chromosomes shown in Figure 20b. What genes for hair and eye color will be in the sperm cells of the man? What genes for hair and eye color will be in the egg cells of the woman?

Now use your models to show how chromosomes in all the possible sperm and egg cells can unite to form all the zygotes possible with respect to hair and eye color. How many different phenotypes are possible among the offspring? Do any of the possible offspring have the same phenotype as their parents? Do any have the same genotype as their parents?

Now extend your model to two chromosomes. Assume that a cleft chin is the result of a gene C that is dominant to the gene for a non-cleft chin, c. Assume, too, that the gene for dimpled cheeks (P) is dominant to the gene (p) for undimpled cheeks. Finally, assume these genes for chin and cheek features are linked on a chromosome other than the chromosome that carries the genes for eye and hair color.

Use pipe cleaners or twisties to represent chromosomes and small pieces of colored yarn to represent genes. Then prepare models of all the possible "chromosome" types and combinations that might be found in the cells of a man who has gray eyes, light brown hair, dimpled cheeks, and a non-cleft chin. Next, prepare models of all the possible "chromosome" types and combinations that might be found in the cells of a woman who has gray eyes, light brown hair, undimpled cheeks, and a cleft chin.

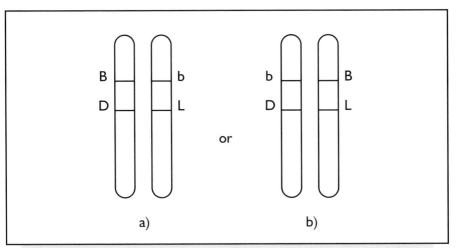

Figure 20. Chromosomes for the hypothetical linked genes for hair color (D and L) and eye color (B and b).

What chromosomes carrying genes for hair color, eye color, chin features, and cheek features can be found in the sperm cells of the man? What genes for hair color, eye color, chin features, and cheek features will be in the egg cells of the woman?

Use your models to show how the chromosomes in all the possible sperm and egg cells can unite to form all the zygotes possible with respect to hair color, eye color, chin features, and cheek features. How many different phenotypes are possible among the offspring? Do any of the possible offspring have the same phenotype as their parents? Do any have the same genotype as their parents?

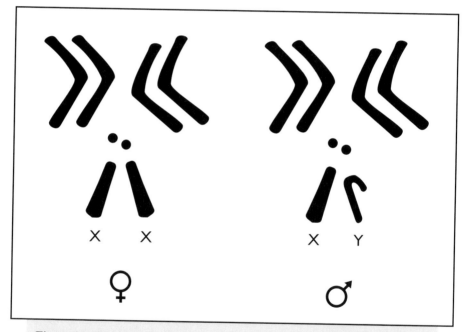

Figure 21. The chromosomes found in female fruit flies are shown on the left. Those found in males are shown on the right. Both have four pairs of chromosomes. But in males the chromosomes in one pair are not similar in appearance. The hook-shaped chromosome is found only in males. It is called the Y chromosome. The other member of the pair, the X chromosome, appears as an identical pair in females.

Sex Determination

When a woman has a baby, the first question asked is usually, Is it a boy or a girl? There were many old theories about how the sex of an offspring is determined. Some maintained it was due to the phase of the moon at the time of conception or the age of the parents. Some believed an offspring's sex depended on whether the egg came from the right or the left ovary or whether the egg was implanted on the right or left side of the uterus. Others, who held that the male parent determined a baby's sex, said it depended on whether the sperm came from the right or the left testicle.

The true explanation came from a microscopic examination of the chromosomes in fruit flies. Geneticists noticed that one pair of chromosomes in male fruit flies was different from that in female flies (see Figure 21). Later it was discovered that in humans the chromosomes in one of the 23 pairs differ in shape. Again, it was the males who had the dissimilar chromosome, which came to be known as the Y chromosome. Thus, females in both fruit flies and humans have two X chromosomes, while males have one X and one Y chromosome. In some species, the male has no Y chromosome, but simply one X chromosome. In other species, such as many birds, moths, and fish, it is the female who has the odd-shaped chromosome.

4-2
A Model of Sex Determination

Who determined your sex? Was it your father or your mother? To find out, place two pipe cleaners or twisties side by side on a sheet of paper as shown in Figure 22a. These two pipe cleaners or

Things you will need:
- eight pipe cleaners or twisties
- paper

twisties represent the two X chromosomes in the cells of your mother. On another sheet of paper, place two more pipe cleaners or twisties. Bend one of these pipe cleaners or twisties as shown in Figure 22a to represent the Y chromosome found paired with an X chromosome in the cells of your father.

During meiosis (see Chapter 2), only one member of each pair of chromosomes enters the gametes (eggs or sperm cells) produced in the ovaries or testes. To form a model of the process, replicate each of the chromosomes by placing another identical "chromosome" in contact with each of those on the two sheets of paper (Figure 22b). These chromosomes then separate to form two new cells (place on separate sheets of paper, as shown in Figure 22c). This is followed by a second cell division without chromosome replication (see Figure 22d) so that each gamete receives only one chromosome from the pair.

How many X chromosomes are in each egg cell? (Actually, only one of the four cells develops. It receives most of the cytoplasm. The other three, known as polar bodies, receive very little cytoplasm and do not survive.)

What fraction of the sperm cells receive an X chromosome? What fraction receive a Y chromosome?

Now use your model to follow the X and Y chromosomes when an egg and a sperm cell unite to form a zygote. Is it the male gamete or the female gamete that determines the sex of the offspring?

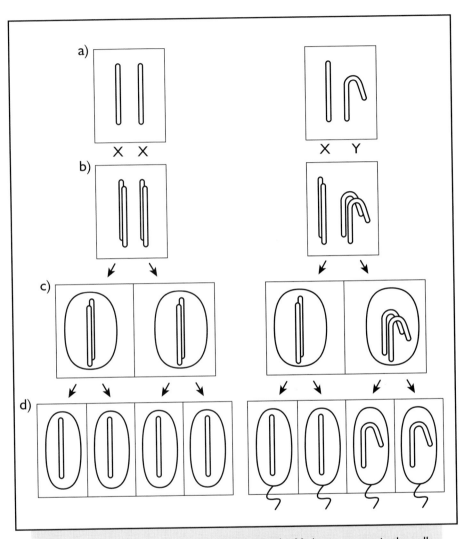

Figure 22. a) The two unbent strips represent the X chromosomes in the cells of your mother. The bent strip represents the Y chromosome in the cells of your father. b, c, d) During meiosis as gametes form, the cells divide twice and each gamete receives only one member of each pair of chromosomes. Each egg receives an X chromosome. Half the sperm cells receive an X chromosome. The other half receive a Y chromosome.

Sex-Linked and Sex-Influenced Traits in Humans

Normally, when a person's skin is cut, platelets in the bloodstream break up and release substances that cause the blood to clot and stop the bleeding. In some people the platelets fail to work properly, and if one of these people suffers even a minor scratch, he can bleed to death. The condition, called hemophilia, affects one in 10,000 males and is a genetic disorder. It can be treated today with injections of a blood-clotting protein. But before medical treatments for hemophiliacs were developed, males with the disorder seldom lived to reproduce. Although a rare disorder, hemophilia became well known because it plagued several European royal families.

Hemophilia is very rare among women. The gene that causes a person to be a hemophiliac is located on the X chromosome. As Figure 23a reveals, women can carry the recessive gene for hemophilia and transmit it to their sons, who will have a 50:50 chance of receiving the gene. Women can also pass the gene to their daughters, who, in turn, can transmit the disorder to their sons. Men who have hemophilia can pass the gene to their daughters but not to their sons. Their sons receive the Y chromosome from their father, and it carries very few genes.

Figure 23b shows the potential offspring in the case of a marriage involving the very rare instance of a hemophilic woman. If she marries a non-hemophiliac man, all her sons will have the disorder because she has the defective gene on both her X chromosomes. What do you know about the father of such a woman? What do you know about her mother?

Figure 24a is a pedigree for a family in which a number of males were hemophiliacs. What do you know about the genotypes of their mothers? Figure 24b shows a rare pedigree in which women had hemophilia.

Hemophilia is one of several disorders that are sex-linked in humans. In all recessive sex-linked genes, the frequency of the abnormality is much higher in males than in females. Since sex-linked genes are found on the X chromosomes, males, who have only one X chromosome, cannot carry a second gene that could mask the effect. Females do have a second X chromosome and so a dominant gene on one chromosome will prevent the recessive gene from being expressed.

Color blindness is the most common sex-linked inherited human trait. It and hemophilia are the best known, but there are more than twenty inherited human traits that are known to be sex-linked. Duchenne dystrophy, a rare disease that destroys muscle fibers, strikes one in 10,000 boys. It has not been found in girls, perhaps because a double dose of the gene is lethal. Other human sex-linked traits include eye defects, such as optic atrophy, and skin disorders, such as the absence of sweat glands. These defects are uncommon

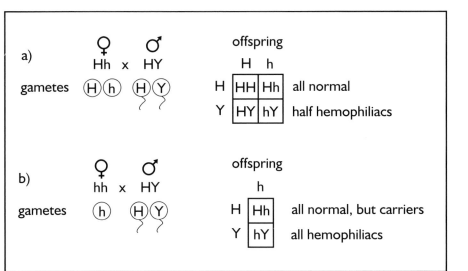

Figure 23. Because the recessive gene for hemophilia (h) is on the X chromosome, a non-hemophiliac woman who carries the gene can expect to transmit the disorder to half her sons. The Y chromosome they receive from their father carries no gene for the disorder. b) Although extremely rare, a woman may have hemophilia. All her sons will have hemophilia and all her daughters will be carriers. The daughters can expect half their sons to be hemophiliacs.

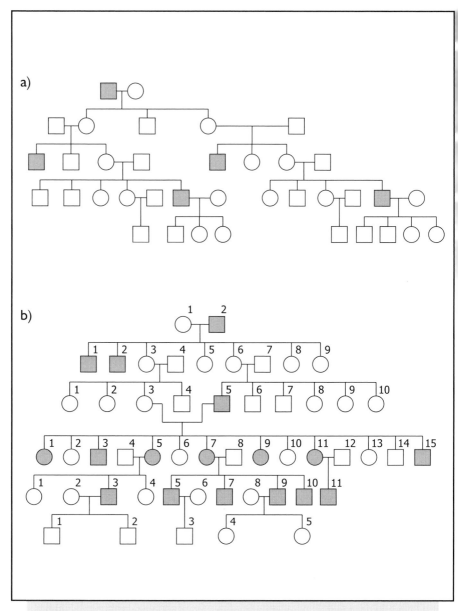

Figure 24. a) A pedigree for a family in which some males have hemophilia. Those with the disorder are indicated by the dark squares. What do you know about the mothers of these hemophiliacs? b) A rare pedigree in which five women in the same generation had hemophilia.

in females; the presence of a dominant gene on their second X chromosome hides the recessive gene.

Just because a trait is far more common in males, or limited to males, does not mean it is sex-linked. Some genes are sex-limited: they appear only in one sex. These include the genes that produce secondary sex characteristics. Heavy beards are generally limited to men. The expression of the gene requires the presence of male sex hormones. However, the gene can be transmitted from mother to son. The trait does not appear in women because women lack the sex hormones required for the gene to be expressed.

A phenotype that is limited to males in a pedigree may be the result of chance. This is particularly true if only a small number of people are involved in the study.

4-3*
A Sex-Linked Trait in Humans

Some people cannot distinguish colors, usually red and green. Color blindness, which affects 8 percent of males, is a sex-linked trait. One test for color blindness involves a word or number made from small greenish and bluish circles that is embedded in a background of reddish and orangish circles.

Things you will need:
- sheet to test for color blindness
- people in your family or a friend's family who are red-green color-blind
- pen or pencil
- notebook

People who are red-green color-blind cannot see the word or number because they have trouble distinguishing between reds and greens. Such test sheets, available from science supply houses (see List of Suppliers), can sometimes be found in science text books. Your school's science department may have such a book or test sheet that you can borrow.

Use the test for color blindness to see if any members of your family or a friend's family are red-green color-blind. Once you have identified a number of people in a family who are color-blind, try to collect enough evidence to show that red-green color blindness is a sex-linked trait.

Exploring on Your Own

Boys who have Duchenne dystrophy die before they reach maturity. Why then does the gene for this disease not become eliminated from the population?

What evidence would you need to show that a gene is transmitted by the Y chromosome? Do some research to find out if any Y-linked genes are known.

In some cases people possess more or less than the usual number of X or Y chromosomes. What are the effects of the following genotypes with respect to X and Y chromosomes: XXX,

XXY, XYY, XXXX, XXXXY, XXYY, XO (only one X and no Y chromosome)?

What are Barr bodies and how are they related to X chromosomes?

Can you find any evidence to indicate that the genes for light-colored eyes and hair are linked?

4-4
The Inheritance of the Length of Index Fingers

Index fingers can be long or short (see Figure 25). A short index finger is shorter than the ring finger. A long index finger is as long as the ring finger. Some claim the trait is sex-linked and that more males than

Things you will need:

• as many related people as possible from your family and other families

• pen or pencil

• notebook

females have short index fingers. Collect data from your own and/or other families where some family members have long index fingers and others have short ones. Does length of the index finger appear to be a sex-linked trait? Is it due to a dominant gene? If not, what, if anything, do your data indicate about the inheritance of this feature?

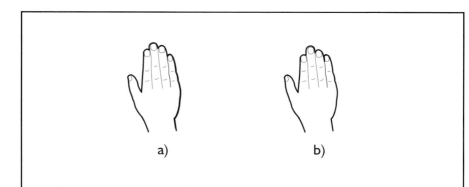

a)   b)

Figure 25. a) Some people have long index fingers, as long as or longer than their ring fingers. b) Others have short index fingers, shorter than their ring fingers.

4-5*
Gender and Probability

A man and a woman marry and have three children. Each child receives an X chromosome from its mother and either an X or a Y chromosome from its father.

Things you will need:

• pen or pencil

• notebook

What is the probability that they will all be boys (all receive a Y chromosome from their father)? What is the probability that they will all be girls (all receive an X chromosome from their father)? Assume that the probability of a baby being a boy or a girl is the same. The first child could be male or female. The same is true of the second and the third. This means there are eight possible combinations: two for the first child, two for the second, and two for the third (2 x 2 x 2 = 8). Figure 26 shows the eight possibilities. What is the probability that all three children will be boys? What is the probability that all three children will be girls?

Now consider a man and woman who have four children. Off the top of your head, what combination of boys and girls do you think is most probable—2 and 2, 3 and 1, or 4 and 0? Next, list all 16 possibilities in a manner similar to Figure 26. Which combination is the most probable? Did you expect what you got?

Exploring on Your Own

The probability for the birth of boys and girls is not really exactly 1:1. Which sex is more likely to be born? Can you explain why? Are the expected life spans the same for both sexes?

What is the origin of the symbols for male and female ($\male$, $\female$)?

Chromosomal Aberrations and Genetic Defects and Diseases

Sometimes chromosomes behave in abnormal ways. For example, they may fail to separate during meiosis. This results in a chromosomal aberration known as nondisjunction. Nondisjunction explains why some human males are born with an extra X chromosome. A male who is XXY has a condition known as Klinefelter's syndrome. He has male sex organs but is usually sterile. A female with three X chromosomes (XXX) is often called a super female. She is often quite tall, usually sterile, and frequently mentally retarded.

People born with Down's syndrome have an extra chromosome on the twenty-first pair due to nondisjunction. Down's syndrome is

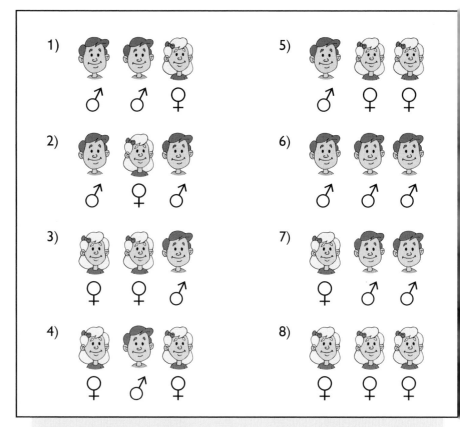

Figure 26. The eight possibilities for gender combinations in families with three children. The circle with an arrow is the symbol for male; the circle with the cross is the symbol for female.

usually characterized by some degree of mental deficiency together with a pattern of physical traits. People with Down's syndrome are usually short and have stubby fingers and a large round head. The fact that children with Down's syndrome are more likely to be born to older women suggests that nondisjunction is age-related.

Another chromosomal aberration associated with one form of Down's syndrome is translocation. Occasionally, someone with Down's syndrome has the usual 46 chromosomes rather than 47. In such cases, however, one chromosome is very large. The increased size is caused by the addition (translocation) of the extra twenty-first chromosome to a member of another pair. Translocations are frequently seen in fruit fly chromosomes.

You have already read about sex-linked disorders such as hemophilia, Duchenne's dystrophy, and red-green color blindness. These disorders are the result of a recessive gene on the X chromosome that has no corresponding gene on the Y chromosome. Huntington's disease (HD) and Marfan's syndrome are transmitted by dominant genes. Huntington's disease causes deterioration of the nervous system. Victims gradually lose control of their muscles and their ability to remember and reason. Slowly, they become unable to speak, walk, or swallow. After 15 to 20 years of deterioration, they die. People who carry the gene can be identified by a careful examination of the tip of chromosome number 4.

People with Marfan's syndrome are nearsighted, tall, and have long fingers. But the most harmful effect, a weakness of the aortic wall (the major artery carrying blood from the heart), is unseen. If the aortic wall gives way, the victim quickly bleeds to death.

Diseases resulting from recessive genes include sickle-cell anemia, cystic fibrosis, Tay-Sachs disease, and phenylketonuria (PKU).

Sickle-cell anemia is so named because it causes red blood cells to become spearlike, clogging small blood vessels. This reduces the oxygen supply to body cells and results in pain, fatigue, and a weakened heart. This disease is most prevalent among Africans and those of African descent.

Cystic fibrosis is most common among whites of European descent. The disease is the result of a defective gene on chromosome number 7. The gene normally produces an enzyme that controls the movement of salt and water in and out of cells in the lungs, pancreas, and intestines. The symptoms associated with cystic fibrosis appear early in life. They include numerous colds and lung infections; thin, greasy feces; and a thick mucus in the lungs that must be removed daily. Patients also receive antibiotics and a dietary supplement that includes the pancreatic enzymes that fail to reach the intestine through clogged pancreatic ducts. Research on corrective gene therapy is under way.

Victims of Tay-Sachs disease, mostly Eastern European Jews, suffer from a defective gene that fails to manufacture a protein that controls fatty deposits in the brain. As a result, fat collects in the brain cells and kills them. The first effects are seen when a baby is about four months old. The child stops its development and its nerve cells begin to die. Such children usually die of pneumonia by the time they are five years old.

PKU is caused by a defective gene that is unable to make an enzyme that changes one chemical (phenylalanine) to another (tyrosine). The accumulation of phenylalanine can result in severe mental retardation. It is now possible to test infants for PKU and to prevent its effects with proper diet.

Exploring on Your Own

In Turner's syndrome, a girl inherits only one X chromosome. It can come from either her father or her mother. Does it matter from which parent she receives the chromosome? David Skuse, a research psychiatrist at the Institute of Child Health in London, thinks it does. Do you?

What is gene therapy and what difficulties are associated with it?

What is the difference between in vivo and ex vivo gene therapy?

What is genetic counseling and how may it prevent the transmission of harmful genes?

What is eugenics? What is euthenics?

Some people believe Abraham Lincoln had Marfan's syndrome. Why would they think so?

5

The Chemistry of Genes

Early in the twentieth century, scientists realized that the genes that control the development and traits of an organism are located on chromosomes. But they did not know the chemical makeup of genes or how they work. During the second half of that century, the chemistry of genes was determined, and scientists discovered the way genes function.

Genes, a Mold, and Enzymes

During the early 1940s, George W. Beadle (1903–1989) and Edward L. Tatum (1909–1975) carried out a series of experiments using a simple mold, *Neurospora crassa*. Their experimental results shed the first light on how genes work. Beadle and Tatum found that ordinary *N. crassa* spores (the reproductive units of mold) could grow on a simple medium that contained only sugar, salts, and biotin (a vitamin). From these simple chemicals, the mold could manufacture all the substances it needed to carry on its life processes.

The scientists X-rayed the mold and then placed its spores on the medium. Many of these spores did not grow on the medium.

Beadle and Tatum hypothesized that those spores that did not grow had undergone a mutation (a change in a gene) that prevented them from making some essential protein or vitamin.

It is known that 20 amino acids are essential in making the proteins found in living cells. Beadle and Tatum used that knowledge to test their hypothesis. They placed X-rayed mold spores on a medium that contained all 20 essential amino acids. In such a complete medium, most of the spores grew. To find out which amino acid or vitamin a mutant spore could not live without, they added various supplements to the simple medium until they found the one that allowed the spores to grow.

Beadle and Tatum believed that the X-rayed spores could not produce some needed amino acid because they lacked an enzyme, a substance that helps a cell to work. The cells instead depended on the medium for the substance. The manufacture of each enzyme, they argued, was controlled by a specific gene. If that gene changed (mutated), the mold could not make the enzyme. Without the enzyme, the mold was unable to make one of the amino acids essential for life. The notion that each gene is associated with the manufacture of a specific enzyme became widely accepted.

Genes, DNA, and the Electron Microscope

Scientists were certain by this time that all genes, like the ones that controlled the mold enzymes, were located on chromosomes. And chemists had found that chromosomes contained proteins and a substance called DNA (deoxyribonucleic acid).

With the development of the electron microscope, it became possible to magnify objects a million times, a thousand times more than with ordinary microscopes. With such magnification, biologists, at last, were able to see the structure of the most basic cells of living matter.

Watson, Crick, and DNA

In 1953, James Watson and Francis Crick published their molecular model of DNA and the means by which it replicated (made a copy of itself). The model of DNA they developed (see Figure 27) was a long, two-stranded, curved ladder known as a double helix; that is, a double spiral. The DNA molecule contained four different kinds of nucleotides, the basic units of nucleic acid. Each nucleotide unit consists of a sugar (deoxyribose), a phosphate group, and a nitrogen-containing base. The sides of the ladder are the sugar and phosphate portions of the molecules, which are joined in a long chain. The sides of the ladder are connected by four bases that constitute the rungs of the ladder. The four bases are thymine, guanine, adenine, and cytosine.

Chemists who had analyzed DNA found that the number of molecules of adenine (A) and thymine (T) within the DNA were always equal. They found, too, that the number of cytosine (C) and guanine (G) molecules were always equal, but not equal to the number of thymine or adenine molecules. Based on that data, Watson and Crick concluded that in DNA's long, double helix-shaped molecule, the C and G bases were always bonded to one another. Similarly, the A and T bases were bonded to one another. So if a portion of one strand of the molecule has the bases ACTG, the corresponding portion of the adjacent strand will have the bases TGAC.

The bonds between the bases A and T or C and G that hold the strands of the double helix together are relatively weak. As a result, at the time of cell division, the strands can separate. Each strand then combines with nucleotides floating about in the cytoplasm to create a duplicate of the strand from which it separated (Figure 28). The result is two identical double helix molecules. Each molecule has a new strand and an old strand. The DNA replicates just as chromosomes replicate. In fact, as you might suspect, a chromosome consists of DNA wound around a protein framework.

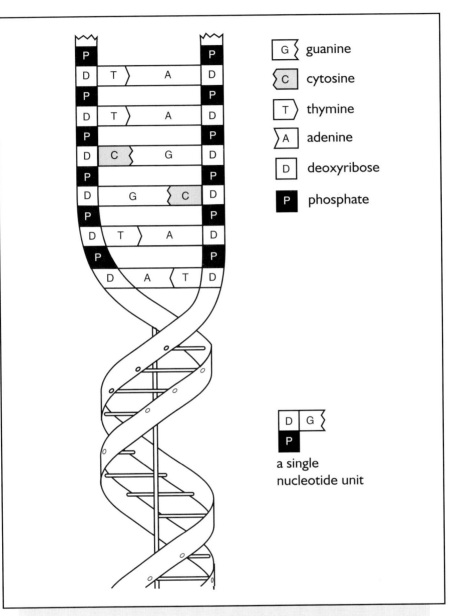

Figure 27. Watson and Crick's model of DNA is a double helix similar to a spiral ladder. Two strands of ribose sugar and phosphate groups constitute the sides. The rungs are made of pairs of nitrogen-containing bases. Adenine is always paired with thymine, and guanine always joins with cytosine.

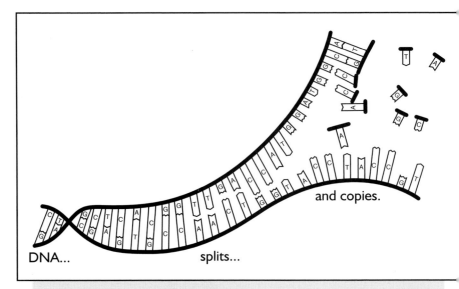

DNA...   splits...   and copies.

Figure 28. During cell division, the DNA strands unzip and replicate by adding nucleotides to build new strands on each of the old ones.

From DNA to Genes

Watson and Crick's model explains the structure of DNA and how it replicates during cell division. But where are the genes? And how do they control the production of proteins, including the enzymes that govern the chemical reactions within cells? What code do they use?

Proteins are long chains of different amino acids joined together. The four bases (C, G, T, and A) alone cannot be the code for joining amino acids together because there are 20 different essential amino acids and only four bases. Even combinations of two bases cannot provide the code, because four bases, taken two at a time, can combine in only 16 different ways (see Figure 29). However, four bases combined three at a time would provide 64 different combinations, more than enough to code for the 20 different amino acids.

96

Using electron microscopes, scientists found that proteins are made on tiny structures called ribosomes that lie outside the nucleus in living cells. But DNA is inside a cell's nucleus. How could genes found in the DNA in the nucleus code for proteins manufactured in a cell's cytoplasm, outside the nucleus?

Experiments showed that RNA (ribonucleic acid), which is very similar to DNA, is found both inside and outside the nucleus of a cell. RNA exists as single rather than double strands of nucleotides. RNA molecules are shorter than those of DNA, and they contain the base uracil (U) in place of thymine (T). During the formation of RNA, U, not T, bonds with A.

The code used in making proteins consists of groups of three bases; these groups are known as codons. The possible codons and the specific amino acids for which they code are shown in Figure 30. There are 64 possible codons but only 20 essential amino acids. As a result, more than one codon may code for an amino acid (see Figure 30). Some codons, such as UAA, UAG, and UGA, are used to signal an end to a chain of amino acids. AUG is sometimes used to signal the start of a protein as well as the production of the amino acid methionine.

	A	T	C	G
A	AA	AT	AC	AG
T	TA	TT	TC	TG
C	CA	CT	CC	CG
G	GA	GT	GC	GG

Figure 29. There are sixteen ways that four bases, taken two at a time, will code for amino acids.

As shown in Figure 31, a form of RNA known as messenger RNA (mRNA) is made on a segment of DNA. The segment is a gene that provides the code for making a particular protein. The mRNA carries the genetic code through the nuclear membrane to the ribosomes in the cytoplasm. Another type of RNA, known as transfer RNA (tRNA), consists of short strands of nucleotides that carry specific amino acids to the ribosomes. There, the amino acids are assembled according to the codons on the mRNA to form the amino

First Letter	Second Letter				Third Letter
	U	C	A	G	
U	Phenylalanine Phenylalanine Leucine Leucine	Serine Serine Serine Serine	Tyrosine Tyrosine Stop Stop	Cysteine Cysteine Stop Tryptophan	U C A G
C	Leucine Leucine Leucine Leucine	Proline Proline Proline Proline	Histidine Histidine Glutamine Glutamine	Arginine Arginine Arginine Arginine	U C A G
A	Isoleucine Isoleucine Isoleucine Methionine*	Threonine Threonine Threonine Threonine	Asparagine Asparagine Lysine Lysine	Serine Serine Arginine Arginine	U C A G
G	Valine Valine Valine Valine	Alanine Alanine Alanine Alanine	Aspartic Acid Aspartic Acid Glutamic Acid Glutamic Acid	Glycine Glycine Glycine Glycine	U C A G

* Also frequently a code to indicate where a gene starts on the DNA strand.

Figure 30. The triplet codes (codons) for the 20 essential amino acids. The codes are carried by messenger RNA from the genes on DNA to the ribosomes. (U = uracil; C = cytosine; A = adenine; G = guanine.) For example, the table shows the code for tryptophan is UGG, and that one code for leucine is UUA. What are some other codes for leucine? What is signaled by the code UAG?

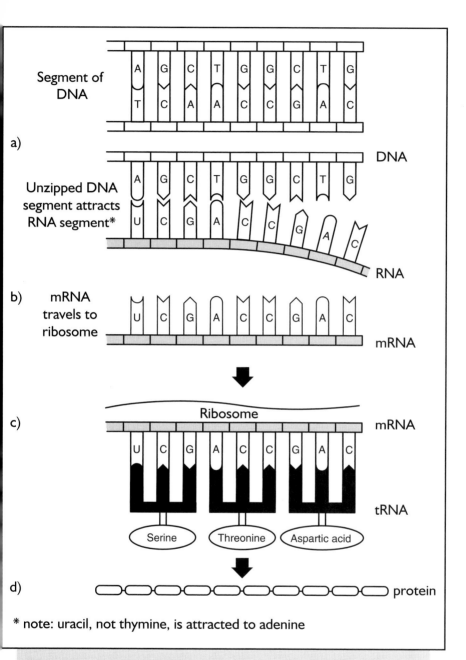

Figure 31. a) A segment of DNA separates from its complement and binds with RNA. b) The RNA segment breaks away as messenger RNA (mRNA) and moves into the cytoplasm, where it attaches to a ribosome. c) There, small units of RNA known as transfer RNA (tRNA) carry specific amino acids to the mRNA. d) The amino acids join to form a protein, which is released. The mRNA is also released and the ribosome is then ready to bind with another mRNA molecule.

acid chains that become protein molecules. The chain continues to grow until a codon that signals Stop is reached on the mRNA. The protein is then released and the mRNA leaves the ribosome.

Sometimes a gene mutates. For example, a cosmic ray may delete a base from the normal sequence of bases in a segment of the DNA. The mRNA produced will then code for a different sequence of amino acids. The result will be a different protein. In rare cases, the new protein may be more beneficial than the old one and the organism will be better able to cope with the environment than other members of the species. In most cases, the new code will fail to produce a protein or it will produce one that is useless or harmful.

5-1
A Three-Dimensional Model of DNA

Using cardboard, heavy wire, scissors, crayons or colored pens, and any other materials that seem appropriate, build a partial model of the DNA molecule. Figure 32 provides useful information, but a three-dimensional model will provide a more realistic picture of the molecule.

Things you will need:
- cardboard
- heavy wire
- scissors
- crayons or colored pens
- other appropriate materials

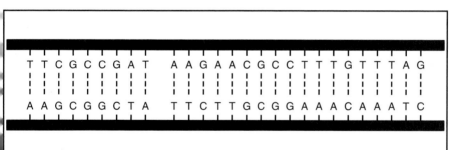

Figure 32. A segment of a DNA molecule is shown. Assume the lower strand with bases AAGC . . . is used to make mRNA. Remember: A = adenine; T = thymine; C = cytosine; and G = guanine. Remember, too, that in RNA, uracil (U), not thymine (T), bonds with adenine (A).

5-2*
Gene Coding and a Mutation

Figure 32 represents a short segment of one strand of DNA. Assume that the lower segment is used to produce part of a messenger RNA molecule.

Things you will need:
• pencil
• notebook

What sequence of bases will be present in the mRNA created on this segment of the DNA? Use U to represent uracil, which, you must remember, bonds with adenine (in place of thymine) in RNA molecules. Use a pencil to record the base sequence in your notebook.

Next, using Figure 32, record the sequence of amino acids (reading from left to right) that tRNA will deliver to the mRNA on a ribosome. What is the significance of the last codon (it should be UAG) on the mRNA?

Suppose a cosmic ray strikes and destroys the base pair at the extreme left-hand end of the DNA shown in Figure 32. What effect will it have on the protein that will be produced by the mRNA and tRNA?

Exploring on Your Own

The hemoglobin protein in the red blood cells of people with sickle-cell anemia differs from normal hemoglobin in just one of the more than 400 amino acids found in the molecule—valine is found where glutamic acid is normally located in the molecule. How can you account for this change?

Sickle-cell anemia, which is carried by a recessive gene, can lead to an early death when the recessive gene is homozygous. Despite its ill effects, it persists, particularly in Africa where it is believed to have originated. How can the gene endure if it has such ill effects?

You know that some genes are dominant and others are recessive. Consider an organism that is heterozygous for some trait. How is the recessive gene repressed from coding during the formation of messenger RNA?

Investigate the work of James Watson and Francis Crick that led them to their model of DNA.

5-3*
A Model to Show How DNA Controls the Making of Proteins

Build a three-dimensional model to show how mRNA is made. Then use the mRNA, together with a model of tRNA, to show how protein molecules are created in the cytoplasm of a cell.

Things you will need:
- cardboard
- heavy wire
- scissors
- crayons or colored pens
- other appropriate materials

Exploring on Your Own

Find out all you can about the Human Genome Project. What benefits are being acquired from this project?

What are marker genes and how are they used?

What is recombinant DNA?

What are transgenic animals?

What is mitochondrial DNA? How is it used to study the evolution of humans?

DNA and Forensic Science

DNA is widely used in forensic science—science used for courtroom debate. Police departments collect hair, blood, and other body materials at crime scenes or from victims. Samples may also be taken from suspects. Crime laboratories perform DNA typing on the samples. Restriction enzymes are used to cut portions of the DNA molecules that differ slightly among humans into fragments of different lengths. Fragments from different sources, such as a victim, a suspect, and evidence left at a crime scene, are placed side by side in a gel and subjected to electrophoresis—an electrical field that attracts the charged portions of the molecules. The smaller particles will move through the gel at a faster rate than the larger ones. Once the electrophoresis is completed, the separated fragments are transferred to a nylon membrane in much the same way that ink is transferred to a blotter. Next, radioactive probes that bind with specific fragments are added to the pattern on the membrane. X-ray film is then placed over the nylon for several days. After the film is developed, bands can be seen on it. The bands are the result of radiation released by the probes that stuck to specific fragments.

By comparing the parallel patterns of bands from the different sources, it is possible to determine whether the DNA could or could not have come from the same individual. A probe producing a match might reveal a DNA type that occurs in one of ten members of a population. But nine matching probes each with an occurrence of one in ten would establish a frequency of one in a billion ($0.1^9 = 0.000000001$). FBI rules for sampling require thirteen matches. Using this same technique, people on death row have been released when DNA evidence proved their innocence.

6

Nature vs. Nurture, Cloning, and Genetic Engineering

The genes we receive from our parents constitute our nature. But how those genes are expressed depends in large measure on the way they are nurtured; that is, on the environment in which they are located.

In this chapter, you will see how environment can affect organisms with identical genotypes. You will also learn how cloning, so common among plants, has been extended to animals and how scientists are finding ways to transfer and replace genes—a process known as genetic engineering.

Nature and Nurture

The genes we are born with, our nature, are not the only factors that affect our growth and development. Environmental or nurturing influences affect us, too. Without proper nourishment, our genes cannot direct the development of our bodies. Without a suitable

106

educational setting, the genes that enable us to think, reason, and learn will languish.

As humans, we inherit genes that allow us to communicate through speech. However, the words and the language we use to communicate depend on where we are born and what we hear. A child born in Beijing will speak Chinese; a child born in Madrid will speak Spanish; a child born in Moscow will speak Russian.

Of course, we cannot purposely subject humans to poor nutrition nor deprive them of an education to see how nurture affects nature. To see how the environment can prevent genes from working properly, we will turn to plants. The seeds you receive in a package for planting are from pure-breeding plants or a cross of pure-breeding plants so that their genes are either identical or nearly so. Consequently, we can be reasonably certain that if we vary environmental conditions, the effects we observe will be due to nurture and not nature.

6-1
Seeds and the Effects of Nurture on Nature

Genes, Plant Growth, and Water

Nearly fill one flowerpot with moist potting soil. Fill a second pot to the same level with dry potting soil. The soil can be dried by leaving it spread out on newspaper in the sun or on a wide, flat pan in an oven at 150°F. Once the soil has cooled, add it to the second pot.

Plant three bean seeds from the same package about one inch deep in each pot. Keep the soil in the first pot damp but not wet. Add no water to the second

Things you will need:

- 10 small flowerpots
- newspaper or flat pan
- an oven
- package of bean seeds
- water
- warm, well-lighted place
- ruler
- notebook
- pen or pencil
- warm, dark place
- well-lighted but very cool place
- different kinds of soil—potting soil, sand, peat, gravel

pot. That soil is to remain dry. Put both pots in a warm, well-lighted place. Continue to water the first pot to keep the soil damp. Watch the pots for several weeks. Do the seeds in either pot germinate? If they do, use a ruler to measure the heights of the plants every other day. Also count and measure the size of their leaves. Record all your data in a notebook. On the basis of your observations and measurements, does water have any effect on the action of the genes found in plant cells?

Genes, Plant Growth, and Light

Nearly fill two flowerpots with moist potting soil. Plant three bean seeds from the same package about one inch deep in each pot. Put one pot in a warm, well-lighted place. Put the second pot in a warm place that is very dark. Add water periodically to keep the soil in both pots damp. Watch both pots for several weeks. Do the seeds in both pots germinate? If they do, use a ruler to measure the heights of the plants every other day. Also count and measure the size of their leaves. What other observation can you make about the plants growing in light as compared with those growing in darkness? Record all your data in a notebook. On the basis of your observations and measurements, does light have any effect on the action of the genes found in plant cells?

Genes, Plant Growth, and Temperature

Nearly fill two flowerpots with moist potting soil. Plant three bean seeds from the same package about one inch deep in each pot. Put one pot in a warm, well-lighted place. Put the second pot in a place that is well lighted and very cool, but not freezing (not below 0°C, or 32°F). Watch the pots for several weeks and keep the soil in both pots moist. Do the seeds in either pot germinate? If they do, use a ruler to measure the heights of the plants every other day. Also count and measure the size of their leaves. Record all your data in a notebook. On the basis of your observations and measurements, does temperature have any effect on the action of the genes found in plant cells?

Genes, Plant Growth, and Soil

Does the type of soil in which seeds are planted affect their germination? To find out, fill four flowerpots with different kinds of soil. Put potting soil in one pot, sand in a second, peat in a third, and gravel in a fourth. The soils should be kept damp but not too wet. Plant three bean seeds, all from the same package, about an inch deep in each pot. Put all the pots in a warm, well-lighted place.

In those soils where seeds germinate, use a ruler to measure the heights of the plants every other day. Also count and measure the size of their leaves. Record all your data in a notebook. In which soils do the seedlings grow into mature plants?

Measure the heights and count the leaves on the plants in the various soils every other day until they mature (produce flowers). Record your data in a notebook. Compare the growth rates and the number of leaves on the plants in the different soils. Are there soils in which the plants thrive? Are there soils in which the plants die or grow poorly? On the basis of your observations and measurements, does the type of soil in which plants grow have any effect on the action of the genes found in plant cells?

Cloning

Cloning, the reproduction of an organism identical to its parent, is common among single-celled animals and plants. For example, one amoeba simply divides to become two amoebas. In that process, the cell's nucleus divides and the chromosomes in the nucleus reproduce themselves during mitosis. As a result, each of the two cells receives the same chromosomes and genes that were in the original cell. Consequently, the two new cells are genetically identical to the original cell.

Plants often reproduce by self-pollination or by vegetative means. When a plant reproduces by vegetative means, a whole new plant will grow from a leaf or part of a stem that is placed in moist soil. Because such plants are genetically identical to their parents, they are clones.

Human identical twins are clones in the sense that they share identical genes. However, their genes are not the same as those of either parent. Identical twins form when a zygote divides into two cells that separate. Each cell then divides over and over again to form two separate, but genetically identical, embryos.

In an attempt to obtain cows that are better milk producers, scientists worked with a cow that was a superior milk producer. After fertilization, they separated the few cells that existed soon after the zygote began to divide. (Such cells will not have yet differentiated, so each cell will divide many times to form an embryo.) Each cell from the pre-embryo was then implanted in the uterus of another cow, who later gave birth to the calf into which the cell grew. As a result, several calves carrying half a superior cow's genes could be produced instead of just one.

Such calves received half their genes from the bull whose sperm was used to fertilize the original cow's egg. Until recently, it was thought that an actual clone—a genetic identical—of a superior cow, or any mammal for that matter, was impossible. But then came Dolly!

In 1996, Ian Wilmut, a Scottish embryologist, worked with an adult ewe (female sheep) and produced a clone that was named Dolly. He took the nucleus of a cell from the ewe's udder and used it to replace the nucleus of an egg from another sheep. The egg was then placed in the uterus of yet another ewe, who eventually gave birth to a lamb (Dolly). Dolly was the clone of the ewe whose udder cell provided the DNA in the nucleus that was transplanted into the egg.

Ordinarily, the DNA in the nucleus of a cell that has become specialized, such as the cells in a sheep's udder, cannot give rise to undifferentiated cells. Normally, undifferentiated cells form as a zygote divides into the cells of an early-stage embryo. Later, the embryo's cells become differentiated into various body tissues, such as muscles, nerves, skin, and so on.

Dr. Wilmut discovered that by "starving" udder cells, he could make their nuclei behave as if they were the nuclei of egg cells. When the DNA of an udder cell that had been starved was used to replace the DNA in an egg cell, it took over the role usually played by the egg cell's chromosomes.

After the cloning of Dolly, Japanese scientists removed the nuclei of eggs from ordinary cows. They then transplanted the DNA from the mammary cells of superior cows into those eggs. The eggs were then inserted into the uteri of surrogate cows, who later gave birth to the clones of the superior cows. These same Japanese scientists later used mammary cells in the milk produced by a cow as it gives birth to produce two clones of the mother cow. This painless technique makes it easier to clone superior cows.

In 1997 a woolly mammoth that had died and been frozen for more than 20,000 years was found by a hunter in Siberia. Scientists hope to extract DNA from one of the animal's cells and insert it into an elephant's egg, just as Dr. Wilmut did with a sheep's egg. The egg will then be implanted in the elephant's womb, where it may grow into a woolly mammoth and be born. If this experiment fails, and if the mammoth is a male, the scientists will try to extract frozen sperm cells and use them to try to fertilize the egg of an elephant. This experiment assumes that a mammoth and an elephant, like a mare and a jackass, can produce a hybrid offspring. (A female horse [mare] mated to a male ass [jack] will give birth to a mule. Mules, however, are sterile, probably because the chromosomes of a mare and a jack are not equal in number or size.)

6-2*
Cloning, Food, and Humans

Gather a small group of friends who have read about and studied the cloning of plants and animals. Once you are together, discuss the following questions about cloning as openly and objectively as possible. Take notes and draw conclusions from what you hear.

Things you will need:

- a group of people who have read about and studied cloning and its implications
- pen
- notebook

- We have the the ability to clone super cows that produce an abundance of milk or meat. It is also possible to clone other animals that provide humans with meat, wool, eggs, and other food. Should animals be cloned? What effect may cloning have on the ability to feed the world's population, which now exceeds six billion people?

- Would it be possible to clone humans? If it were possible, should it ever be done? What are the pros and cons?

Exploring on Your Own

Suggest to your school's debating coach that the cloning of humans might serve as a topic for debate. Then provide the team with material both pro and con.

Genetic Engineering

Early in the 1970s, Stanley Cohen, at Stanford University, was able to separate plasmids from a common bacteria, *Escherichia coli* (*E. coli*), which is found in human intestines. (Plasmids are donutlike loops of DNA found in the bacteria's cytoplasm.) Cohen put the plasmids in a solution that contained restriction enzymes. The enzymes cut the plasmids at specific places.

He also used restriction enzymes to separate genes from the chromosomes of a species of African toads. The genes were then mixed with the broken plasmids from the *E. coli*. Ligase, an enzyme. that "glues" DNA pieces together, was added. The result was a plasmid chimera—a plasmid that contained DNA from two different organisms. The modified plasmids entered the bacteria so that the toad genes became part of the *E. coli*'s genetic content and were passed on to succeeding generations as the cells divided.

Using similar techniques, yeast genes were added to *E. coli*, as were genes from other animals, plants, bacteria, and viruses. Because bacteria reproduce rapidly, up to a billion cell divisions per day, bacteria can serve as gene factories. Such factories are now used to produce human insulin that is used by people with diabetes, who are unable to make their own insulin.

Gene therapy researchers are seeking ways to replace defective human genes, such as those that cause cancer and other diseases, with normal genes. Harmless viruses are being used to insert healthy genes into patients' cells. In a recent experiment, genes for human growth hormone were inserted into a mouse embryo. After birth, these mice grew into adults that were twice the size of their parents.

At the Salk Institute for Biological Studies in La Jolla, California, scientists injected the region of a day-old chicken embryo typically destined to become a wing with a virus carrying a gene that normally causes a leg to develop. When this tissue was transferred to other chick embryos, the embryos developed legs where normally they would have formed wings.

Genetic engineering is currently being used to produce a variety of foods that have been genetically altered. For example, genes that suppress the chemical reactions that cause softening have been added to tomatoes. The genetically altered tomatoes now have a shelflife of twenty days.

However, genetic engineering is not without problems. Several years ago, genetic engineers were looking for a way to produce a variety of corn resistant to the corn borer. (This pest causes more than a billion dollars' worth of damage annually to America's corn crop.) They spliced DNA from a species of bacteria that produces a toxin that kills the corn borer into the corn cells' chromosomes. The corn then produced the same toxin as the bacteria, making it resistant to corn borers.

Although the toxin has no effect on humans or honeybees, a Cornell entomologist found that it did kill monarch butterflies. Monarch larvae feed exclusively on milkweed leaves. When the entomologist placed pollen from the pest-resistant corn on milkweed, he found that the feeding monarch larvae either died or were stunted. Larvae feeding on uncontaminated milkweed were unaffected. The experiment shows that genetic engineering can have unexpected results. In fact, many consumers refer to genetically modified food as Frankenfood.

Recently scientists at Princeton University used a tiny glass needle to inject a gene into the nucleus of a mouse zygote shortly after fertilization. The zygote was then implanted into the uterus of a mouse. The injected gene carried the code for the production of a chemical that enhances memory and learning. Mice born with the added gene produced more of the chemical than usual. These mice—known as Doogie mice after the boy genius in the TV program *Doogie Howser, M.D.*—learned tasks faster and remembered what they had learned better than normal mice. Furthermore, they were able to transmit their added "intelligence" to their offspring.

These experiments with mice have implications for humans. However, as one psychiatrist pointed out, it's a long leap from mouse learning to human learning. Learning which lever to push to receive food is very different from understanding algebra, philosophy, or even genetics.

Glossary

ABO blood types—Classification of human blood based on the presence of antigens A and B in the red blood cells. Type AB blood has both antigens; type O blood has neither antigen.

adenine—One of the four organic bases found in DNA.

amino acids—Molecules that are the building blocks of proteins.

anaphase—A stage in mitosis in which the chromosomes are being pulled apart.

chromosomal aberrations—Abnormal behavior of chromosomes such as nondisjunction or translocation.

cloning—The reproduction of an organism identical to its parent.

codon—A group of three nucleotides on RNA that codes for certain amino acids.

color blindness—Inability to distinguish between or among two or more colors.

cystic fibrosis—A disease related to a defective gene on chromosome number 7 that results in a failure of salt and water to move in and out of lung cells.

cytoplasm—The portion of a cell that surrounds the nucleus.

cytosine—One of the four organic bases found in DNA.

diploid number—The number of chromosomes in a body cell or in a germ cell that gives rise to gametes prior to meiosis.

DNA (deoxyribonucleic acid)—A nucleic acid that has deoxyribose as its sugar component. It is found in chromosomes.

dominant gene—A gene that produces its effect whether homozygous or heterozygous.

Down's syndrome—A genetic defect that results in mental deficiency accompanied by a number of physical traits such as short stature, stubby fingers, large tongue, and round head. Most people with this condition have three number 21 chromosomes instead of two.

Drosophila melangaster—A species of fruit fly widely used in genetic research.

egg—The female gamete.

enzyme—A substance, usually a protein, that speeds up chemical reactions in cells. A gene, found on a chromosome, provides the code for making each enzyme.

F_1—The first filial generation; the offspring of a parent who is homozygous for the dominant gene of a particular trait mated to a parent homozygous for the recessive gene for the same trait.

F_2—The second filial generation; the offspring of F_1 individuals mated together.

gamete—A sperm or egg cell. These cells have the haploid number of chromosomes.

gene—The basic unit of inheritance; a segment of the DNA molecule within a chromosome. Genes provide the chemical codes needed to make proteins.

guanine—One of the four organic bases found in DNA.

haploid—Having a single set of unpaired chromosomes. In humans the gamete is haploid following meiosis.

hemoglobin—An iron-containing compound found in red blood cells.

hemophilia—A disorder in which blood does not clot normally.

Huntington's disease—A fatal disease caused by a dominant gene. It is characterized by involuntary movements of the arms and legs and mental deterioration; these symptoms begin to appear in middle age.

linked genes—Genes that are on the same chromosome and, therefore, tend to stick together rather than separate at random when they enter gametes.

Marfan's syndrome—A disorder in which those affected are nearsighted, abnormally tall, have long fingers, and a weakness of the aortic wall.

meiosis— A type of cell division in which the paired chromosomes are reduced to single chromosomes in the gametes formed during the process.

messenger RNA (mRNA)—RNA that is made as a copy of a segment of DNA within the nucleus. It can travel to ribosomes within the cytoplasm, where it serves as a chemical code for assembling amino acids into protein.

metaphase—A stage in meiosis and in mitosis when the chromosomes are lined up side by side.

mitosis—A type of cell division in which chromosomes replicate and separate so that each new or daughter cell has the same diploid number of chromosomes as the parent cell.

mutation—A chemical change in a gene or a structural change in a chromosome.

nondisjunction—A chromosomal aberration in which the chromosomes fail to separate during meiosis or fail to divide in meiosis or mitosis.

pedigree—An inheritance record (a family tree) usually seen as a diagram showing relationships among individuals.

phenylketonuria (PKU)—A genetic defect that can lead to severe mental retardation unless a proper diet is maintained from early in life.

phenylthiocarbamide (PTC)—A chemical substance that has a bitter taste to some people and no taste to others, depending on their genotype.

prophase—The stage in cell division when the nuclear membrane disappears, spindle fibers appear, and chromosomes become tightly coiled.

proteins—Large molecules made from long chains of amino acids.

recessive gene—A gene that produces its effect only when it is homozygous. In the heterozygous condition its effect is hidden by the dominant gene with which it is paired.

ribosomes—Tiny particles in the cytoplasm of a cell that serve as sites for making protein. Messenger RNA attaches to these ribosomes.

RNA (ribonucleic acid)—A nucleic acid that has ribose rather than deoxyribose as its sugar component. It is found in both the nucleus and the cytoplasm of cells.

sex chromosomes—The X and Y chromosomes. Human females have two X chromosomes; males have one X and one Y chromosome.

sex-linked genes—Genes found either on the X or the Y chromosome.

sickle-cell anemia—A disease in which red blood cells become sickle-shaped, which causes the blood to lose its ability to carry oxygen.

sodium benzoate—A salt that some people can taste and others cannot.

sperm—The male gamete.

Tay-Sachs disease—A disease caused by a defective gene that results in the collection of fat in the brain cells, causing them to die. Children with this disease usually die of pneumonia at an early age.

telophase—The final stage of mitosis in which chromosomes are clustered at opposite sides of a cell and a new cell membrane is forming between them.

thiourea—A bitter chemical that some people can taste and others cannot.

thymine—One of the four organic bases found in DNA.

transfer RNA (tRNA)—A type of RNA that is coded for a specific amino acid and attaches it to the protein being formed.

translocation—A chromosomal aberration in which a piece of one chromosome becomes attached to another part of the same chromosome or to a chromosome of a different pair.

uracil—One of the organic bases found in RNA but not in DNA.

X chromosome—A chromosome found singly in male body cells and doubly in female body cells.

Y chromosome—A chromosome generally found only in males.

zygote—A cell formed by the union of a sperm and egg.

List of Suppliers

Carolina Biological Supply Co.
2700 York Road
Burlington, NC 27215
(800) 334-5551
http://www.carolina.com

**Connecticut Valley Biological
Supply Co., Inc.**
82 Valley Road, Box 326
Southampton, MA 01073
(800) 628-7748

Delta Education
P.O. Box 915
Hudson, NH 03051-0915
(800) 258-1302

Edmund Scientific Co.
101 East Gloucester Pike
Barrington, NJ 08007
(609) 547-3488

Educational Innovations, Inc.
362 Main Avenue
Norwalk, CT 06851
http://www.teachersource.com

Fisher Science Education
4500 Turnberry
Hanover Park, IL 60133
(800) 955-1177
http://www.fisheredu.com/

Frey Scientific
100 Paragon Parkway
Mansfield, OH 44903
(800) 225-3739

Nasco-Fort Atkinson
P.O. Box 901
Fort Atkinson, WI 53538-0901
(800) 558-9595

Nasco-Modesto
P.O. Box 3837
Modesto, CA 95352-3837
(800) 558-9595
http://www.nascofa.com/prod/Home

Sargent-Welch/VWR Scientific
P.O. Box 5229
Buffalo Grove, IL 60089-5229
(800) SAR-GENT
http://www.SargentWelch.com

Science Kit & Boreal Laboratories
777 East Park Drive
Tonawanda, NY 14150
(800) 828-7777
http://sciencekit.com

Ward's Natural Science Establishment, Inc.
P.O. Box 92912
Rochester, NY 14692-9012
(800) 962-2660
http://www.wardsci.com

Further Reading

Aronson, Billy. *They Came From DNA.* New York: W. H. Freeman, 1993.

Balkwill, Fran. *DNA Is Here to Stay.* Minneapolis: Carolrhoda Books, 1993.

Barr, George. *Science Research Experiments for Young People.* New York: Dover, 1989.

Bochinski, Julianne Blair. *The Complete Handbook of Science Fair Projects.* New York: John Wiley & Sons, 1996.

Bombaugh, Ruth J. *Science Fair Success, Revised and Expanded.* Springfield, N.J.: Enslow Publishers, Inc., 1999.

Bornstein, Sandy. *What Makes You What You Are: A First Look at Genetics.* New York: Julian Messner, 1989.

Brynie, Faith Hickman. *Genetics & Human Health.* Brookfield, Conn.: Millbrook Press, 1995.

Edelson, Edward. *Genetics and Heredity.* New York: Chelsea House Publishers, 1991.

————. *Oxford Portraits in Science: Gregor Mendel and the Roots of Genetics.* New York: Oxford, University Press, 1999.

Gardner, Robert. *Science Fair Projects—Planning, Presenting, Succeeding.* Springfield, N.J.: Enslow Publishers, Inc., 1999.

————. *Science Projects About Plants.* Springfield, N.J.: Enslow Publishers, Inc., 1999.

Gutnik, Martin J. *Genetics Projects for Young Scientists.* New York: Franklin Watts, Inc., 1985.

Harris, Jacqueline L. *Hereditary Diseases.* New York: Twenty-First Century Books, 1993.

Jefferis, David. *Cloning: Frontiers of Genetic Engineering.* New York: Crabtree, 1999.

Krieger, Melanie Jacobs. *How to Excel in Science Competitions, Revised and Updated.* Springfield, N.J.: Enslow Publishers, Inc., 1999.

Markle, Sandra. *The Young Scientist's Guide to Successful Science Projects.* New York: Lothrop, Lee, and Shepard, 1990.

Tocci, Salvatore. *How to Do a Science Fair Project, Revised Edition.* Danbury, Conn.: Franklin Watts, Inc., 1997.

Internet Addresses

Manning, Gerard. *The WWW Virtual Library:* Drosophila. October 6, 2000. <http://ceolas.org/fly/> (December 8, 2000).

Morano, David. *Cyber-Fair*. "Experimental Science Projects: An Introductory Level Guide." May 27, 1995. <http:www.isd77. k12.mn.us/resources/cf/SciProjIntro.html> (December 8, 2000).

United States Department of Energy. *Human Genome Project Information*. November 20, 2000. <http://www.ornl.gov/hgmis> (December 8, 2000).

ThinkQuest. *The Gene School*. n.d. <http://library.thinkquest.org/ 19037/heredity.html> (December 8, 2000).

Index

A

adenine, 94
agglutination, 65–66
amino acids, 91, 97, 98
antibodies, 65–66
antigens, 65–66
Aristotle, 13

B

base pairs, 94, 96
Beadle, George W., 92–93
beards, 84
blood types
    A, B, AB, O, 65–67, 68–70
    determining, 66–67
    inheritance of, 68–70
    M, N, MN, 67
    Rh, 67, 68

C

chromatin, 34
chromosomal aberrations,
    87–90
chromosomes, 34–35, 37, 38,
    39–41, 42, 44–45, 71
cleft chin, 62
cloning, 110–112
codons, 97–98, 100
color blindness, 81, 84
Crick, Francis, 94
cystic fibrosis, 89–90
cytosine, 94

D

Darwin, Charles, 15
de Maupertuis, Pierre-Louis, 14
de Vries, Hugo, 33
dimples, 62
DNA, 7, 93
    and chromosomes, 94
    double helix, 94
    and forensic science, 105
    and genes, 96–98, 100
    models, 94–104
    and proteins, 96–97, 100,
        102, 104
    three-dimensional model,
        101
Dolly, 111
Down's syndrome, 88–89
Duchenne dystrophy, 81, 84, 89

E

earlobes, 62
egg cells, 7, 15, 37, 44
electron microscope, 93, 97
Escherichia coli, 113–114
eye color, 55, 57, 64

F

family tree (pedigrees), 50,
    52–53, 80, 83
    and traits, 55, 57, 59, 60,
        61
    blood type, 68–70
    creating, 56

Flemming, Walther, 34
forensic science, 105
fruit fly (*Drosophila melanogaster*), 45, 46, 71
    body color, 72–73
    diagram, 48
    experiments, 47–49
    life cycle, 46
    linked genes, 72–73
    wing length, 72–73
    and X and Y chromosomes, 77

G
gametes, 19, 37, 40–41, 44, 78
gender and probability, 87
genes, 7, 37, 80–81, 83, 92–93
genetic defects and diseases, 87–90
genetic engineering, 106, 113–114
genotype, 30, 76, 80
guanine, 94

H
hair color, 65
hemophilia, 80–82
heredity
    definition, 7
    of domestic plants and animals, 12–13
    early theories of, 13–14
heterozygous factors, 22
Homo sapiens, 11
homozygous factors, 22
Huntington's disease, 53, 89

I
identical twins, 110
index finger length, 86

inherited traits, 7, 12, 55, 62, 63, 64, 65, 68–70, 86

K
Klinefelter's syndrome, 88

L
linked genes, 71–73, 74–76

M
Marfan's syndrome, 89
meiosis, 37, 78
    microscopic view, 38
    model, 42, 44
    phases, 38
Mendel, Gregor, 15–18, 19, 22, 25, 27, 28, 30, 33–34
mitosis, 34–35, 39–41
    model, 39–41
    phases, 38
Muller, Hermann Joseph, 45
mutations, 33–34, 100, 102–103

N
nature vs. nurture, 106–107
nondisjunction, 88
nucleotides, 94
nucleus, 34, 37

P
pea plants, 15–18, 71
phenotype, 30, 74, 76, 83
phenylketonuria (PKU), 89–90
phenylthiocarbamide (PTC), 58–59
probability
    and gender, 87
    and heredity, 23–25
Punnett square, 19–22, 24, 26, 27, 31

R
Rh factor, 68
RNA, 97–98, 100, 102, 103, 104
rolled tongue, 62
Röntgen, Wilhelm Conrad, 45

S
safety, 9
sex determination, 77, 78
sex-linked traits, 80–81, 83, 84
sickle-cell anemia, 89–90, 102
sodium benzoate, 61
sperm cells, 7, 15, 37, 44, 73

T
tasting, 58–59, 60, 61
Tatum, Edward L., 92–93
Tay-Sachs disease, 89–90
Tetrads, 44
thiourea, 60
thumb shape, 63

thymine, 94, 97
traits
    inherited, 12
    sex-linked, 80–81, 83, 86
    tracing, 55
translocation, 89

U
uracil, 97

W
Watson, James, 94
Wilmut, Ian, 111–112

X
X and Y chromosomes, 77–78, 80–81, 83, 84–85, 86, 87–88
    and sex determination, 77–78
    and super female, 88

Z
zygotes, 15, 35, 37, 44, 76, 78, 110, 115